KU-504-003

kamasutra

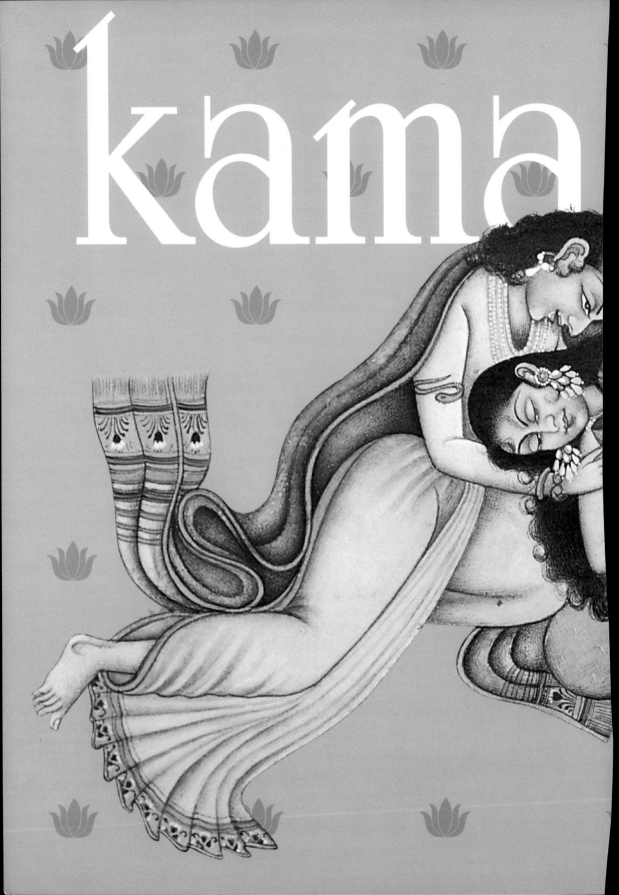

kama

sutra

world's oldest treatise on sex

Tarun Chopra

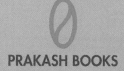

PRAKASH BOOKS

contents

Reprinted 2007 by Prakash Books India Pvt. Ltd.
1, Ansari Road, Daryaganj. New Delhi-110 002, India
Email: sales@prakashbooks.com
Website: www.prakashbooks.com
Tel.: 011-23247062-65

Copyright © 2005 Prakash Books India Pvt. Ltd.
Text & Photographs Copyright © 2005 Tarun Chopra

Designed by: Yogesh Suraksha Design Studio Pvt. Ltd.
www.ysdesignstudio.com

All right reserved. No part of this publication
may be reproduced, stored in a retrieval system
or transmitted in any form or by any means, electronic,
mechanical, photocopying, recording or otherwise,
without the prior permission of the copyright holders.

ISBN: 978-81-7234-087-2

Printed & Bound at Rave India www.raveindiapress.com

introduction

*Passion is expressed
in Indian art and
culture from the time
immemorial.
The carving on the
opposite page shows
the carving from ninth
century Kailasha
temple in Ellora Caves.
Entire temple is carved
out from one single
piece of mountain and
the walls of the temple
are decorated with
narrative carvings*

*(Pages 6-7)
An artist's creation out
of sand on Puri beach
probably inspired by
the sensuous apsaras
of Konarak Temple
close by*

*K*amasutra is perhaps the world's oldest treatise on sex. It is a remarkable document, which gives an insight into social and political ethos of India some 2000 years ago. Indeed, the paucity of written material pertaining to ancient India makes Kamasutra an important source of information for understanding one of the world's oldest living civilizations.

It is truly remarkable that a detailed study of sexual behaviour was done around 4th century AD. What makes the book even more unique is the fact that many of the observations made by the author have withstood the test of time and are practical even today.

Kamasutra derives its name from Kamadevta, the Hindu god of love. The text, parts of which date back to the first century of the Christian era, contains about one thousand two hundred and fifty shlokas or verses, which are divided into seven parts comprising thirty six chapters.

That kama (love /sex) and religion are two sides of the same coin is depicted with great candor in the great Hindu epics. Rig Veda (part of four Vedas or books of knowledge), written 4500 B.C. talk about an elaborate romance between an apsara (celestial dancer) Urvashi and King Pururavas. In Mahabharata, Arjuna resists the designs of lusting apsara. Lord Krishna, eighth incarnation of Lord Vishnu is an epitome of divine lover. His sexual escapades with village maidens (gopis) have been expressed in various art forms such as paintings and dance. And nothing is left to the imagination if one views the ancient temples adorned with what is inaccurately labeled 'erotic art'. It must be understood that in Indian ethos a very fine line divides sex and religion. In fact sexual escapades of the gods are woven into the mythological stories and the rituals of Hindu religion. Erotic tradition manifests itself in explicit sculptures carved on ancient Hindu temples spread all across India. The most famous of these temples are at Khajuraho in central India and Konarak on the eastern coast dating back to the tenth and thirteenth century AD respectively.

(Previous pages) Lord Krishna is the eighth incarnation of Lord Vishnu, the second God of Hindu trinity. In Hindu mythology, he is considered as the ultimate lover. He embodies all sixteen qualities that a man must possess. In paintings he is always surrounded by gopies or village maidens who try to out do each other for his attention. The painting, which decorates the Dutch Palace walls in Cochin, shows Lord Krishna attracting many girls by his melodious flute. Green colour is associated with good in South India

In Vedic times the goals of human life, called purusharaths, were codified. They were divided under four heads - Dharma, Artha, Kama and Moksha. The first three are collectively known as Trivarga, their practice in life shows the way to Moksha, which means liberation of the soul (atman) from the cycle of rebirth.

Out of the three purusharaths, Dharma or righteousness is considered most important, as it is the right conduct of the worldly life in accordance to the laws of nature. Artha stands for collecting worldly comforts and highlights the

introduction

On this page one can see the details of a fifth century wall painting from Ajanta caves. In spite of depicting a thousand years old scene it manages to exude sensuousness of the courtesans that surround the king. The designs of their dresses, hairstyles and ornaments are all vividly depicted

stage of grihasth ashram (the stage of raising a family) during which one accumulates wealth and property.

This book, Kamasutra, dwells on the third purushartha, viz. Kama or sexual pleasure that is central to the evolution of the mankind. Here the law states that a sexual intercourse should be more than just an action to procreate - maximum pleasure should be derived from it. However, it should be enjoyed in moderation.

The original work on Kamasutra is attributed to a high caste Brahmin priest called Mallinga Vatsyayana, who compiled it

Apsaras or the celestial dancers find a prominent place in Indian iconography. Their role in Hindu religion is to entertain the Gods in heaven. Here a tenth century sculpture from Khajuraho temple depicts the sensuous body of an apsara accentuated with big bosom and hips, which are symbols of fertility in India

from the works of Gurus Bhabhravya, Gotamukha and Gonikputra. These gurus, and others are often quoted in the narration of the manuscript.

The first part of the text deals with the location, possession and sensual decoration of the house of the citizen. Details of furniture are well-defined, with a couch for lovemaking, board games on low table, bee-wax candles and aromatic perfumes etc. The second part dwells on various sexual techniques such as petting, kissing, biting and love making. This part of the book is also thoughtful of a woman's needs; it advises the reader how to prepare a woman for a sexual climax, like kneading of the dough before baking it. In case the woman fails to be satisfied than a man should use his finger on her yoni, 'as an elephant rubs his trunk against a tree'. The third section explains the art of seduction of the maiden and fourth section deals with the marriage and setting up the family.

There is a long list of instructions for the woman on how to excel in the role of a wife. The fifth part is devoted to seducing other men's wives, with necessary cautions of dire consequences thrown in. Sixth section is devoted to the courtesans, who till only about a century ago were an important part of the social life of the upper crust. Incidentally, some Hindi films have dealt with these feudal traditions that are fast dying out. In this section of the book the courtesans are candidly advised on how to milk their patrons of their wealth in order to safeguard the future. The seventh, and the last part is devoted to sexual aids and aphrodisiacs. These were important products of the time as they helped to maintain the virility of the sexually active citizen.

After years of remaining confined in just a handful of Sanskrit manuscripts, the Kamasutra of Vatsyayana was first brought to light and translated into English by Sir Richard Burton in 1889. If it weren't for his efforts, this incredible work of literature would have been lost to the world.

In other cultures it is impossible to treat the sensual study without making it appear pornographic. But here, it is treated in a simple, matter of fact sort of way. As Venus was represented by the Greeks as the epitome of beauty in a woman to stand forth as the type of the beauty of woman, for the Hindus it is the Padmini or Lotus woman as the most perfect feminine beauty.

"A woman, in whom the following signs are visible, is called a Padmini.
Her face is pleasing as the full moon; her body, well clothed with flesh,
is soft as the Shiras or mustard flower, her skin is fine,
tender and fair as the yellow lotus, never dark coloured.
Her eyes are bright and beautiful as the orbs of the fawn, well cut,
and with reddish corners. Her bosom is hard, full and high;
she has a good neck; her nose is straight and lovely,
and three folds or wrinkles cross her middle - about the umbilical region.
Her yoni resembles the opening lotus bud, and her love seed (Kama salila)
is perfumed like the lily that has newly burst.
She walks with swan-like gait, and her voice is low and musical
as the note of the Kokila bird, she delights in white raiments, in fine jewels,
and in rich dresses. She eats little, sleeps lightly,
and being as respectful and religious as she is clever and courteous,
she is ever anxious to worship the gods, and to enjoy the conversation of Brahmins.
Such, then, is the Padmini or Lotus woman".

life of a citizen

A person should practice Dharma, Artha and Kama in different stages of his life. It should be done in such a manner that they complement each other and not conflict with one another. Dharma should be learned from the Gurus and religious scriptures. During the brhamcharya or in youth, one should lead the life of a religious student and learn Dharma under the guidance of a guru. In grihastha ashram or as householder one should dedicate oneself to the accumulation of Artha or material wealth, should get married, have children and spend time with friends. The art of earning wealth can be learnt from business people and court officials.

Kama, is the enjoyment of appropriate object, by the five senses of human body, assisted by ones mind and soul. The pleasure, which arises from the contact between the organ of senses and consciousness of pleasure, is called Kama. It can be learned from Kama Shastras (aphorisms of love) or from gurus who are well versed with the subject.

ARTS AND SCIENCES

Young girls should study Kamasutra along with its arts and sciences before marriage, and after it, with the consent of their husbands. Some narrow minded people were not in favour of imparting sex education to girls. But Vatsyayana is of opinion that women already know the practice of Kamasutra, and that practice is derived from the Kama Shastra, or the science of Kama itself. Moreover, it is not only in this but in many other cases that, though the practice of a science is known to all, only a few persons are acquainted with the rules and laws on which the science is based. Persons perform religious duties required of them on auspicious days, which are fixed by astrology, even though they have not studied astrology. Similarly, riders of horses and elephants train these animals without knowing the science of training animals, but from practice only.

A woman should learn the sixty-four practices that form a part of the Kama Shastra from some close friend in private. Her teacher should be one of the following persons: the daughter of a nurse brought up with her and already married, a female friend who can

Singhar or to decorate ones body has been an age old tradition followed by Indian women. Kohl for the eyes, colouring of the lips (using a kind of bark), decorating the body with sandal wood paste and painting hand and feet are some of the decorative elements used till date

This cloth painting known as Pichwai has been executed in Kisangarh style, here the eyes of the maidens are painted as if these were petals of lotus. Here one can see the Lord Krishna's gopies, who are waiting for his amorous advances.

be trusted in everything, or her aunt, or an old female servant, or a female beggar who may have formerly lived in the family, or her own sister who can always be trusted. Trust and confidentiality are an essential condition for learning the art of Kamasutra.

The arts which complement the study of Kamasutra are: Singing, playing the musical instruments, dancing, tattooing, adorning an idol with rice and flowers, colouring the teeth, garments, hair, nails and bodies. Fixing stained glass into a floor, the art of making beds, and spreading out carpets and cushions for reclining, storing and accumulating water, art of cooking, art of sewing, solution of riddles, covert speeches, verbal puzzles and enigmatical questions, the art of mimicry or imitation, reading, including chanting and intoning, practice with sword, single stick, quarter staff and bow and arrow, architecture, or the art of building , knowledge about gold and silver coins, and jewels and gems; art of cock fighting, quail fighting and ram fighting, art of teaching parrots and starlings to speak, art of framing mystical diagrams, of addressing spells and charms.

A public woman, endowed with a good disposition, beauty and other attractive qualities, and also versed in the above arts, obtains the title of a Ganika, or courtesan of high quality. And she receives a

life of a citizen

seat of honour in an assemblage of men, respected by the king, and praised by learned men, and she becomes an object of universal regard. Even the bare knowledge of these arts makes a woman attractive. The daughter of a king, as well as the daughter of a minister, on learning the arts of Kamasutra, can make her husband attracted to her, in spite of him having other wives. If a woman becomes separated from her husband or falls into distress, she can easily support herself by the knowledge of these arts. A man who is brave, well versed in arts, who has gift of the gab, can win over women's regard in little time.

After acquiring the knowledge of Dharma, a man should become a householder and concentrate his energies on becoming prosperous either through inheritance, investments or conquest. He should find a house in a city or a village in a good neighbourhood. It should ideally be located near a source of water. It should be surrounded by a garden, contain two rooms, an outer and an inner one. The females should occupy the inner room, while the outer room, balmy with rich perfumes, should contain a bed with soft mattress, covered with a clean white cloth. It should be low in the middle part with a canopy on top. Two pillows, one at the top, another

Hindu gods are always depicted with their consorts. In this wall painting from the Dutch Palace in Cochin one can see lord Vishnu seated affectionately with Goddess Laxmi. These two paintings show distinct styles of depicting similar themes

The miniature painting on the opposite page shows a village belle, who on seeing that she is alone, sensuously disrobes herself to bathe in the lotus pond. The grove of banana trees and swirling monsoon clouds in the sky add to the excitement in the scene

at the bottom along with garlands and bunches of flowers upon it. There should be also a couch and a stool with fragrant ointments for the night, flower pots containing collyrium and other fragrant substances, such as the bark of the common citron tree for perfuming the mouth. Near the couch, on the ground, there should be a pot for spitting, a box containing ornaments, and also a lute hanging from a peg made of the tooth of an elephant, a board for drawing, a pot containing perfume, some books and some garlands of the yellow flowers. Not far from the couch, there should be a round seat, a toy cart, and a board for playing dice games; outside the outer room there should be cages of birds, and a separate place for spinning and carving. In the garden there should be a whirling swing and a common swing, as also a bower of creepers covered with flowers, in which a raised garden should be made for sitting.

The householder, after waking up in the morning and performed his necessary duties, should wash his teeth, apply a limited quantity of ointments and perfumes to his body, put some ornaments on his person and collyrium on his eyelids and below his eyes, colour his lips with alacktaka (natural colour derived from lac), and look at himself in the mirror. Having then eaten betel leaves, that gives fragrance to the mouth, he should go about his daily business. He should bathe daily, anoint his body with oil every other day, apply a lathering substance to his body every three days (soap was introduced much later by the Muslims in 11th century), get his head (including face) shaved every four days and the other parts of his body every five or ten days. All these things should be done without fail, and the sweat of the armpits should also be removed. Meals should be taken in the morning, in the afternoon and again at night. After breakfast, parrots and other birds should be taught to speak, and the fighting of cocks, quails and rams should follow. Limited time should be devoted to diversions with Pithamardas, Vitas, and Vidushakas. Later one should take siesta. After this the householder, having put on his clothes and ornaments, should converse with his friends. In the evening there should be singing, and after that the householder, along with his friend, should wait in his room, the arrival of the woman that may be attached to him. After her arrival at his house, he and his friend should welcome her and entertain her with a loving and agreeable conversation. Thus end the duties of the day of the householder.

These seventeenth century erotic carvings, executed in wood, adorn the pagoda style temples of the Himalayan region. The reason to put the erotic carvings is to protect the temple from lightning, as the goddess of lightning is a virgin, hence she shies away from graphic depiction of sex

On some particular auspicious day, an assembly of citizens should be convened in the temple. There the singers should compete with each other and finally rewarded on their merit. The members of the assembly should help each other both in good and bad times. Hospitality should be shown to the strangers who have come to the assembly. In the forenoon men should go horse riding in the company of public woman and followed by servants.

When men of the same social standing, age and interests sit together in company with a public woman (courtesan or Veshya was an important element in Hindu society, her education, intellect and beauty were far superior to the women of the household) or in the

assembly or abode of citizens, various mind games, such as completion of verses half composed by the others, testing the knowledge of one another in arts and literature were played. The beautiful woman, who has the power to read the other's mind and who has same interests as other men, is respected in such gatherings. Later the householder should offer alcohol made from flowers, fruits and barks of various trees to the public woman and the citizens should drink with her on such occasions.

"A citizen capable of holding discussions in Sanskrit and other dialects on various topics, earns great respect in the society. The wise should not resort to a society disliked by the public, governed by no rules and intent on destruction of others. But a learned

man living in the society which acts according to the wishes of the people and which has pleasure for its only object is highly respected in the world".

OTHERS' WIVES

When Kama is practised by men of the four classes, according to the rules of the Holy Writ (i.e. by lawful marriage) with virgins of their own caste, it then becomes a means of acquiring lawful progeny and good fame. The practice of Kama with women of the higher castes, those previously enjoyed by others (even though they be of the same caste) is prohibited. But the practice of Kama with Nayikas (women of the lower castes, women excommunicated from their own caste, public women and women twice married) is permitted. The object of practising Kama with such women is pleasure only.

Nayika is any woman who could be enjoyed without sin. The object of women is pleasure and progeny. Any woman who is enjoyed without sin for the purpose of accomplishing either the one or the other of these two objects is a Nayika. The fourth kind of Nayika is neither enjoyed for pleasure or progeny, but merely for accomplishing some especial task at hand.

A woman who has been previously enjoyed by many others, a twice-married woman, women who have powerful, rich and influential husbands can be seduced for one's personal gains. A woman, whose husband has violated the chastity of my wives, should be paid back in the same coin. It is said that any woman who has been enjoyed by five men is a fit and proper person to be enjoyed.

For these and similar other reasons the wives of other men may be enjoyed, but it must be distinctly understood that it is only allowed for special reasons, and not for mere carnal desire.

THE FOLLOWING WOMEN ARE NOT TO BE ENJOYED:

A leper, lunatic, woman turned out of caste, woman who reveals secrets, woman who publicly expresses desire for sexual intercourse, woman who is extremely white, woman who is extremely black, bad-smelling woman, woman who leads the life of an ascetic, lastly the wife of a relation, friend, king and of a learned Brahmin.

A woman should learn the sixty-four practices that form part of Kama Shastra from a close friend in private. Her teacher should be a nurse, friend, elder sister or an old servant who can be trusted. After learning these arts she should practice them with a man well versed in the art of Kamasutra

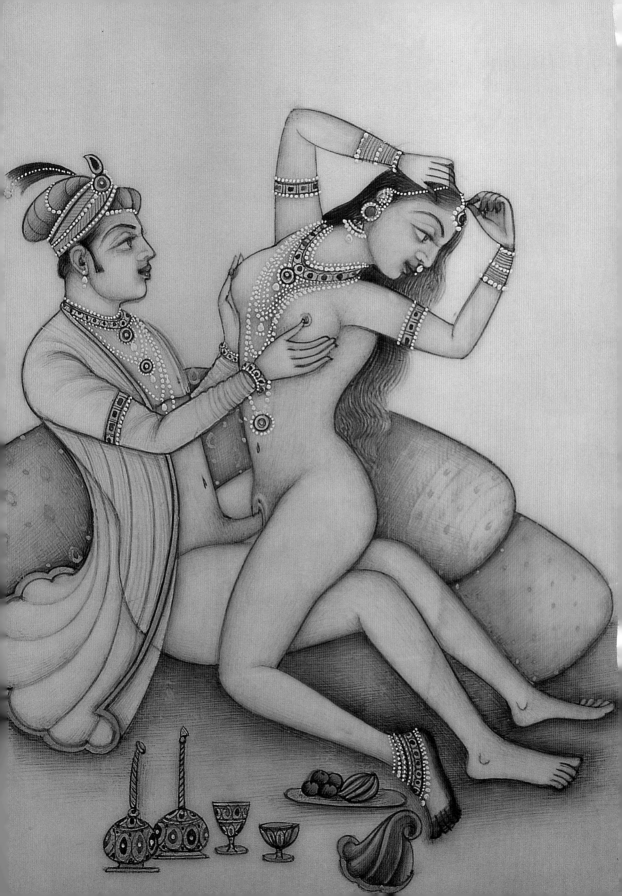

'The man who is ingenious and wise,
who is accompanied by a friend,
and who knows the intentions of others,
as also the proper time and place
for doing everything,
can gain over, very easily,
even a woman who is very hard to be obtained.'

love making

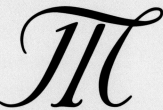

Vatsyayana, the author of Kamasutra, says that there is no fixed place or time for lovemaking. In this painting it is shown with great candour how two pleasures of hunting and sexual union can be combined for joyous results

Man, according to the size of his lingam, is divided into three classes, viz. the hare man, the bull man and the horse man; Woman also, according to the depth of her yoni, is either a female deer, a mare or a female elephant. There are three equal unions between persons of the same size, and there are six unequal unions, in the case where the dimensions are not compatible. In these unequal unions, when the male is bigger than the female in size, his union with a woman next to him in size is called high union, and is of two kinds; while his union with the woman most remote from his size is called the highest union. On the other hand, when the female exceeds the male in size, her union with a man immediately next to her in size is called low union, and is of two kinds; while her union with a man most remote from her in size is called the lowest union, and is of one kind only.

In other words, the horse and mare, the bull and deer, form the high union, while the horse and deer form the highest union. On the female side, the elephant and bull, the mare and hare, form low unions, while the elephant and the hare make the lowest unions.

Amongst all these, equal unions are the best, the highest and the lowest are the worst, and the rest are mediocre, and with them the high are better than the low. High unions are said to be better than low ones, for in the former it is possible for the male to satisfy his own passion without injuring the female, while in the latter it is difficult for the female to be satisfied by any means.

There are also nine kinds of union according to the force of passion or carnal desire, as follows:

A man is called a man of small passion whose desire at the time of sexual union is not great, whose semen is scanty, and who cannot bear the warm embraces of the female. Those who differ from this temperament are called men of mediocre passion, while those of intense passion are full of desire. In the same way, women are supposed to have the three levels of passion. Lastly, according to time one lasts in love-making, there are three kinds

At the time of sexual union the passion of male is intense, and his time short, but in subsequent unions on the same day reverse is the case. For woman, first her passion is weak and time is long, but subsequently her passion is intense and time becomes short

of men and women, the short-timed, the moderate-timed and the long-timed; and of these, as mentioned earlier; here too there are nine kinds of unions. The women differ in regards to the time as described in the following words.

At the first sexual union the passion of the male is intense, and his time is short, but in subsequent unions on the same day the reverse is the case. With the woman, however, it is just the opposite: the first passion is weak, and her time is long, but on subsequent occasions on the same day, her passion is intense and her time short, until her passion is satisfied. Experienced men know that as dough is prepared for baking, so must a woman be prepared for sexual intercourse, for she will enjoy it as much as you do.

Auddalika (Guru of Kama Shastras) says, "Females do not emit as males do. The males simply remove their desire, while the females, from their consciousness of desire, feel a certain kind of pleasure, which gives them satisfaction, but it is impossible for them to tell you what kind of pleasure they feel. The fact from which this becomes evident is, that males, when engaged in coition, cease of themselves after emission, and are satisfied, but it is not so with females."

It takes a long time for women to get aroused; it is during this period of arousal that she enjoys great pleasures, it quite natural for her to egg the lover on to prolong the pleasure.

"By union with men the lust, desire or passion of women is satisfied and the pleasure derived from the consciousness of it is called their satisfaction."

In the beginning of making love the passion of the woman is not intense, and she cannot bear the vigorous thrusts of her lover, but by degrees her passion increases until she ceases to think about her body, and then finally she wishes to stop from going on.

Even in ordinary things that revolve with great force, such as a potter's wheel, or a top, we find that the motion at first is slow, but by degrees it becomes very rapid. In the same way the passion of the woman having gradually increased, she has a desire to discontinue coition.

"The fall of the semen of the man takes place only at the end of coition, while the semen of the woman falls continually, and after the semen of both has all fallen away then they wish for the discontinuance of coition."

The strength of passion with women varies a great deal, some being easily satisfied, and others eager and willing to go on for a long time. To satisfy the woman thoroughly a man must have recourse to art. It is certain that a fluid flows from the woman in larger or smaller quantities, but her satisfaction is not complete until she has experienced the orgasm.

The consciousness of pleasure derived from lovemaking is different between men and women. During sex, men are the actors and women are the persons acted upon. This is because of difference in the physical nature of the male and the female. And from this difference in the ways of working follows the difference in the consciousness of pleasure, for a man thinks, 'I am making love to this woman', and a woman thinks, 'this man is making love to me'. Though both men and women derive pleasure from the act of coition, the way it is brought about is by different means, each individual performing his own work in the matter, irrespective of the other, and each deriving individually their own consciousness of pleasure from the act they perform.

THE EMBRACE

The part of the Kama Shastra, which treats with sexual union, is also called 'sixty-four' (Chatushshashti). This part contains eight subjects, viz. the embrace, kissing, scratching with the nails or fingers, biting, lying down, making various sounds, playing the part of a man and the Auparishtaka or mouth congress. Each of these subjects being of eight kinds, and eight multiplied by eight being sixty-four, this part is therefore named 'sixty-four'.

The embrace which indicates the mutual attraction of a man and woman who have come together is of four kinds: touching, rubbing, piercing and pressing.

When a man under some pretext or other goes in front or alongside of a woman and touches her body with his own, it is called the 'touching embrace'.

When a woman in a lonely place bends down, as if to pick up something, and pierces, as it were, a man sitting or standing, with her breasts, and the man in return takes hold of them, it is called a 'piercing embrace'.

The above two kinds of embrace take place only between

In the beginning of making love the passion of woman is not intense, and she cannot bear the vigorous thrusts of her lover, but by degrees her passion increases until she ceases to think about her body, and then finally her breathing turns into gasping and she asks for more

love making

persons who are getting to know each other. When the story gets better the following embraces come in play.

When two lovers are walking slowly together, either in the dark or in a lonely place and rub their bodies against each other, it is called a 'rubbing embrace'.

When on the above occasion one of them presses the other's body forcibly against a wall or pillar, it is called a 'pressing embrace'.

When men and women are in love, their embraces are a bit more graphic and are termed as: the twining of a creeper, or climbing a tree, or the mixture of sesame seed with rice, or milk and water embrace.

When a woman, clinging to a man as a creeper twines round a tree, bends his head down to hers with the desire of kissing

When a woman kneels
on her fours, with
support from cushions
or pillows, and her
lover mounts her like
a bull, it called the
congress of the cow.
The lover should
make sure that the
yoni is moist and
prepared for
penetration;
man should hold her
from the thighs or
breasts and keep
pulling her towards
him in gentle rhythms

him, embraces him, and looks lovingly towards him, it is called an embrace like the 'twining of a creeper'.

When a woman, places one of her feet on the foot of her lover and the other on one of his thighs, passes one of her arms round his back, and the other on his shoulders, and climbs up on him in order to kiss, it is called an embrace like the 'climbing of a tree'.

When lovers lie on a bed and embrace each other so closely that the arms and thighs are encircled by one another, this is called an embrace like 'the mixture of sesame seed with rice'.

When a man and a woman are deeply in love with each other and embrace each other as if they were entering into each other's bodies, while the woman is sitting on the lap of the man, then it is called an embrace like a 'mixture of milk and water'. Sesame seed and rice plus milk and water embrace take place at the time of sexual union.

When one of two lovers presses forcibly one or both of the thighs of the other between his or her own, it is called the 'embrace of thighs'.

When a man presses the jaghana or middle part of the woman's body against his own, and mounts upon her to practice, either scratching with the nail or finger, or biting, or striking, or kissing, the hair of the woman being loose and flowing, it is called the 'embrace of the jaghana'.

When a man places his breast between the breasts of a of woman and presses her with it, it is called the 'embrace of the breasts'.

When either of the lovers touches the mouth, the eyes and the forehead of the other with his or her own, it is called the 'embrace of the forehead'.

'The whole subject of embracing is of such a nature that men who ask questions about it, or who hear about it, or who talk about it, acquire thereby a desire for enjoyment. Even those embraces that are not mentioned in the Kama Shastra should be practiced at the time of sexual enjoyment, if they are in any way conducive to the increase of love or passion. The rules of the Shastra apply so long as the passion of man is middling, but when the wheel of love is once set in motion, there is then no Shastra and no order.'

KISSING

As mentioned in the end of the last chapter, there is no fixed time or order between the embrace, the kiss, and the pressing or scratching with the nails or fingers, but all these things should be done before sexual union takes place, while striking and making the various sounds generally takes place at the time of the union. Vatsyayana, however, thinks that anything may take place at any time, for love does not care for time or order.

On the occasion of the first congress, kissing, embracing and massaging should be done moderately and alternately. On subsequent occasions, however, the reverse of all this may take place, and moderation will not be necessary, they may continue for a long time and, for the purpose of kindling love, they may be all done at the same time.

The following are the places for kissing: the forehead, the eyes, the cheeks, the throat, the bosom, the breasts, the lips, and the interior of the mouth. Other areas of interest for kissing on a women body are: the joints of the thighs, the arms and the navel.

Types of kisses employed by the young girls are: nominal kiss, throbbing kiss and the touching kiss.

When a girl only touches the mouth of her lover with her own, but does not herself do anything, it is called the 'nominal kiss'. When a girl, setting aside her bashfulness a little, wishes to touch the lip that is pressed into her mouth, and with that object moves her lower lip, but not the upper one, it is called the 'throbbing kiss'. When a girl touches her lover's lip with her tongue, and having shut her eyes, places her hands on those of her lover, it is called the 'touching kiss'.

Other variations of the kiss are: The straight kiss, the bent kiss, the turned kiss and the pressed kiss. When the lips of two lovers are brought into direct contact with each other, it is called a 'straight kiss'. When the heads of two lovers are bent towards each other, and when so bent, kissing takes place, it is called a 'bent kiss'. When one of them turns up the face of the other by holding the head and chin, and then kissing, it is called a 'turned kiss'. Lastly when the lower lip is pressed with much force, it is called a 'pressed kiss'.

love making

When a woman,
clinging to a man as a
creeper twines round
the tree, bends his
head down to hers
with a desire of kissing
him and looks lovingly
towards him,
it is called 'embrace of
twining of a creeper'

There is also a fifth kind of kiss called the 'greatly pressed kiss', which is effected by taking hold of the lower lip between two fingers, and then, after touching it with the tongue, pressing it with great force with the lip.

To initiate kissing, a game could be played between the couple as to who will get hold of the lips first. If the woman loses, she should pretend to cry, should keep her lover off by shaking her hands, and turn away from him and dispute with him saying, 'lets begin another game'. If she loses this a second time, she should appear doubly distressed, and when her lover is off his guard or asleep, she should get hold of his lower lip, and hold it in her teeth, so that it should not slip away, and then she should laugh, dance about, ridicule him in a joking way. Such are the games and quarrels as far as kissing is concerned, but the same may be applied with regard to the pressing or scratching with the nails and fingers, biting and striking. All these however are only peculiar to men and women of intense passion.

When a man kisses the upper lip of a woman, while she in return kisses his lower lip, it is called the 'kiss of the upper lip'. When one of them takes both the lips of the other between his or her own, it is called 'a clasping kiss'. A woman, however, only takes this kind of kiss from a man who has no moustache. And on the occasion of this kiss, if one of them touches the teeth, the tongue, and the palate of the other, with his or her tongue, it is called the 'fighting of the tongue'. In the same way, the pressing of the teeth of the one against the mouth of the other is to be practised.

Kissing is of four kinds according to the different parts of the body which are kissed, for each part of the body requires different kind of kiss. When a woman looks at the face of her lover while he is asleep and kisses it to show her intention or desire, it is called a 'kiss that kindles love'. When a woman kisses her lover while he is engaged in business, or while he is quarrelling with her, or while he is looking at something else, so that his mind may be turned away, it is called a 'kiss that turns away'.

When a lover coming home late at night kisses his beloved, who is asleep on her bed, in order to show her his desire, it is called a 'kiss that awakens'. On such an occasion the woman may pretend to be asleep at the time of her lover's arrival,

Man according to the size of his lingam (phallus) is divided into three classes viz. the hare man, the bull man and the horse man; woman according to the depth of her yoni (vagina) is also divided into three classes, a female deer, a mare or a female elephant. The three equal unions of the persons of the same size are considered to be the best

so that she may know his intention and obtain respect from him. When a person kisses the reflection of the person he loves in a mirror, in water, or on a wall, it is called a 'kiss showing the intention'.

When a person kisses a child sitting on his lap, or a picture, or an image, or figure, in the presence of the person beloved by him, it is called a 'transferred kiss'.

When at night at a theatre or in an assembly of caste men, a man coming up to a woman kisses a finger of her hand if she be standing, or a toe of her foot if she be sitting, or when a woman rubs her lover's body, places her face on his thigh (as if she was sleepy) so as to inflame his passion, and kisses his thigh or inside it, it is called a 'demonstrative kiss'.

"Whatever things may be done by one of the lovers to the other, the same should be returned by the other, i.e. if the woman kisses him he should kiss her in return, if she strikes him he should also strike her in return."

LOVE BITES

When love becomes intense, pressing with the nails or scratching the body with them is practised, and it is done on the following occasions: on the first visit; at the time of setting out on a journey; on the return from a journey; at the time when an angry lover is reconciled; and lastly when the woman is intoxicated.

Pressing with the nails is not a usual thing except with those who are intensely passionate, i.e. full of passion. It is employed, together with biting, by those to whom the practice is agreeable.

The ideal places for the purpose are the arm pit, throat, breasts, lips, jaghana or middle parts of the body, and the thighs. When the impetuosity of passion is excessive, the places need not be considered.

When a person presses the chin, the breasts, the lower lip, or the jaghana of another so softly that no scratch or mark is left, but only the hair on the body becomes erect from the touch of the nails, it is called a 'sounding or pressing with the nails'. This is used in the case of a young girl when her lover massages her, scratches her head, and wants to trouble or frighten her. The

When a deer woman raises her thighs and keeps them wide apart and engages in congress, it is called 'the yawning position'. This position facilitates the entrance of lingam bigger in size compared to her yoni

love making

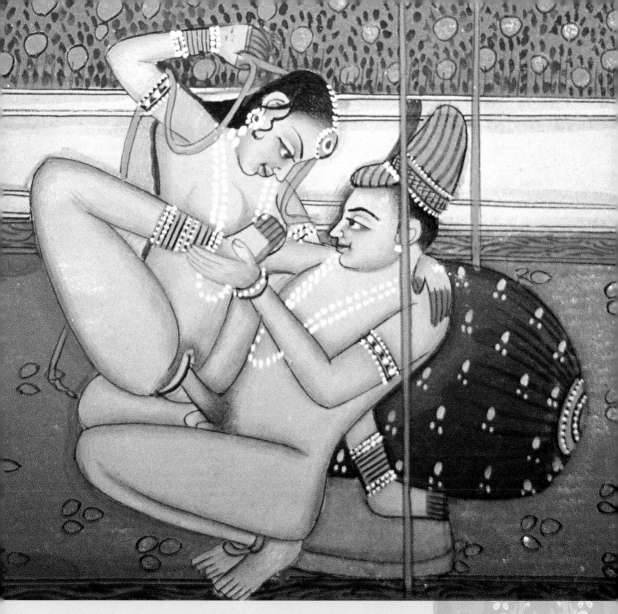

curved mark with the nails, which is impressed on the neck and the breasts, is called the 'half moon'. When the half moons are impressed opposite to each other, it is called a 'circle'. This mark with the nails is generally made on the navel, the small cavities about the buttocks, and on the joints of the thigh. A mark in the form of a small line, and which can be made on any part of the body, is called a 'line'. This same line, when it is curved, and made on the breast, is called a 'tiger's nail'. When a curved mark is made on the breast by means of the five nails, it is called a 'peacock's foot'. This mark is made with the object

of being praised, for it requires a great deal of skill. When five marks with the nails are made close to one another near the nipple of the breast, it is called 'the jump of a hare'. A mark made on the breast or on the hips in the form of a leaf of the blue lotus is called the 'leaf of a blue lotus'. When a person is going on a journey, and makes a mark on the thighs, or on the breast, it is called a 'token of remembrance'. On such an occasion three or four lines are impressed close to one another with the nails.

The marks of the nails should not be made on married women, but particular kinds of marks may be made on their private parts for the remembrance and increase of love.

'The love of a woman who sees the marks of nails on the

love making

When the female raises both her thighs straight up into the air with her man supporting them, it is called the 'rising position'.

(Facing page) If a man fails to satisfy his lover in an unequal union, he should then concentrate on rubbing the woman's breasts, and with his lingam he should rub the yoni 'as an elephant rubs his trunk against a tree'.

private parts of her body, even though they are old and almost worn out, becomes again fresh and new. If there be no marks of nails to remind a person of the passages of love, then love is lessened in the same way as when no union takes place for a long time.'

Even when a stranger sees at a distance a young woman with the marks of nails on her breast (before the advent of Islam women in India were dressed very sensually) he is filled with love and respect for her. A man who carries the marks of nails and teeth on some parts of his body, inflames passion in the mind of a woman, however unyielding she might be, as the nail and bite marks are triggers of desire.

love making

ON BITING

All the places that can be kissed are also the places that can be bitten, except the upper lip, the interior of the mouth, and the eyes. The qualities of good teeth are as follows: They should be equal, possessed of a pleasing brightness, capable of being coloured, of proper proportions, unbroken, and with sharp ends.

The bite, which is shown only by the excessive redness of the skin, is called the 'hidden bite'. When the skin is pressed down on both sides, it is called the 'swollen bite'. When a small portion of the skin is bitten with two teeth only, it is called the 'point'. The lower lip is the place on which the 'hidden bite', the swollen bite', and the 'point' are made; When such small portions of the skin are bitten with all the teeth, it is called the 'line of points'. When the teeth and the lips are employed together in biting, is called the 'coral and the jewel'. The lip is the coral, and the teeth the jewel.

The 'swollen bite' and the 'coral and the jewel' bite are done on the cheek. When biting is done with all the teeth, it is called

love making

The complicated love positions are practiced for total control resulting in bliss. The woman may act the part of a man to satisfy her desire for novelty. The man should anoint his lingam with herbal mixture to have hypnotic effect on his partner. The scene of sexual energy, carved in sand stone, dates back to tenth century and decorates the walls of Laxmana Temple in Khajuraho

the 'line of jewels'. Both the 'line of points' and the 'line of jewels' are to be impressed on the throat, the arm pit, and the joints of the thighs; but the 'line of points' alone is to be impressed on the forehead and the thighs.

The bite, which consists of unequal risings in a circle, and which comes from the space between the teeth, is called the 'broken cloud'. The ideal place for this bite is on firm breasts. The biting, which consists of many broad rows of marks near to one another, with red intervals, is called the 'biting of a boar'. This is impressed on the breasts and the shoulders; and these two last modes of biting are peculiar to persons of intense passion. Kissing, pressing with the nails, and biting are the ornaments that should be done on the left cheek only.

In the affairs of love a man should do such things as are agreeable to the women of different regions.

The women of the Balhika country are gained over by striking. The women of Avantika are fond of foul pleasures and do not have good manners. The women of the Maharashtra are fond of practising the sixty-four arts, they utter low and harsh words, and like to be spoken to in the same way, and have an

impetuous desire of enjoyment. The women of Pataliputra (i.e. the modern Patna) are of the same nature as the women of the Maharashtra, but show their likings only in secret. The women of the Dravida country, though they are rubbed and pressed about at the time of sexual enjoyment, have a slow fall of semen, that is, they are very slow in the act of coition.

The women of Varanasi are moderately passionate, they go through every kind of enjoyment, cover their bodies and abuse those who utter low, mean and harsh words. The women of Avanti hate kissing, marking with the nails, and biting but they have a fondness for various kinds of sexual union. The women of Malwa like embracing and kissing, but not wounding, and they are gained over by striking. The women of Abhira, and those of the country about the Indus and five rivers (i.e. the Punjab), are gained over by the Auparishtaka or mouth congress. The women of Aparatika are full of passion, and make slowly the sound 'Sit'. The women of the Lat country have even more impetuous desire, and also make the sound 'Sit'.

The women of the Stri Rajya, and of Koshola (Oude), are full of impetuous desire, their semen falls in large quantities and they are fond of taking medicine to make it do so. The women of the Andhra country have tender bodies, they are fond of enjoyment, and have a liking for voluptuous pleasures.

The nature of a particular person, should be understood. There can be no generalization about how to go about making love.

Among the things mentioned above, viz. embracing, kissing, etc., those which increase passion should be done first, and those which are only for amusement or variety should be done afterwards.

'When a man bites a woman forcibly, she should angrily do the same to him with double force. Thus a "point" should be returned with a "line of points", and a "line of points" with a "broken cloud", and if she be excessively chafed, she should at once begin a love quarrel with him. At such a time she should take hold of her lover by the hair, and bend his head down, and kiss his lower lip, and then, being intoxicated with love, she should shut her eyes and bite him in various places. Even by day, and in a place of public resort, when her lover shows her

During love making when the man lifts the middle part of his body and the woman turns around her middle part, the position is called 'the swing'. It can be achieved only after lot of practice

Before leaving on a long journey, man should put bite marks on the body of his lover so that she can remember his passion during his absence

When two lovers meet, after a long period of separation on account of travelling or after a quarrel, then the union arising after such absence is called the loving congress. It is carried out according to the liking of the lovers and as long as they choose

any mark that she may have inflicted on his body, she should smile at the sight of it, and turning her face as if she were going to chide him, she should show him with an angry look the marks on her own body that have been made by him. Thus if men and women act according to each other's liking, their love for each other will not be lessened even in one hundred years.'

IDEAL POSITIONS FOR COSMIC ORGASM

On the occasion of a 'high congress' the Mrigi (Deer) woman should lie down in such a way as to widen her yoni, while in a 'low congress' the Hastini (Elephant) woman should lie down so as to contract hers. But in an 'equal congress' they should lie down in the natural position. What is said above concerning the Mrigi and the Hastini applies also to the Vadawa (Mare) woman. In a 'low congress' the woman should particularly make use of medicine, to cause her desires to be satisfied quickly.

love making

The Deer woman has the following three ways of lying down:

When she lowers her head and raises her middle parts, it is called the 'widely opened position'. At such a time the man should apply some ointment, so as to make the entrance easy.

When she raises her thighs and keeps them wide apart and engages in congress, it is called the 'yawning position'.

When she places her thighs with her legs doubled on them upon her sides, and thus engages in congress, it is called the position of Indrani and this is learnt only by practice. The position is also useful in the case of the 'highest congress'.

The 'clasping position' is used in 'low congress', and in the 'lowest congress', together with the 'pressing position', the 'twining position', and the 'mare's position'. When the legs of both the male and the female are stretched straight out over each other, it is called the 'clasping position'. It is of two kinds, the side position and the supine position, according to the way in which they lie down. In the side position the male should invariably lie on his left side, and cause the woman to lie on her right side,

and this rule is to be observed in lying down with all kinds of women. When, after congress has begun in the clasping position, the woman presses her lover with her thighs, it is called the 'pressing position'. When the woman places one of her thighs across the thigh of her lover it is called the 'twining position'. When a woman forcibly holds in her yoni the lingam after it is in, it is called the 'mare's position'. This is learnt by practice only and is chiefly found among the women of the Andhra country.

When the female raises both of her thighs straight up, it is called the 'rising position'. When she raises both of her legs, and places them on her lover's shoulders, it is called the 'yawning position'. When the legs are contracted, and thus held by the lover before his bosom, it is called the 'pressed position'. When only one of her legs is stretched out, it is called the 'half pressed position'.

When the woman places one of her legs on her lover's shoulder, and stretches the other out, and then places the latter on his shoulder, and stretches out the other, and continues to do so alternately, it is called the 'splitting of a bamboo'. When one of her legs is placed on the head, and the other is stretched out, it is called the 'fixing of a nail'. This is learnt by practice only.

When both the legs of the woman are contracted, and placed on her stomach, it is called the 'crab's position'.

When the thighs are raised and placed one upon the other, it is called the 'packed position'. When the shanks are placed one upon the other, it is called the 'lotus-like position'. When a man, during congress, turns round, and enjoys the woman without leaving her, while she embraces him round the back all the time, it is called the 'turning position', and is learnt only by practice.

When a man and a woman support themselves on each other's bodies, or on a wall, or pillar, and thus while standing engage in congress, it is called the 'supported congress'. When a man supports himself against a wall, and the woman, sitting on his hands joined together and held underneath her, throws her arms round his neck, and putting her thighs alongside his waist, moves herself by her feet, which are touching the wall against which the man is leaning, it is called the 'suspended congress'.

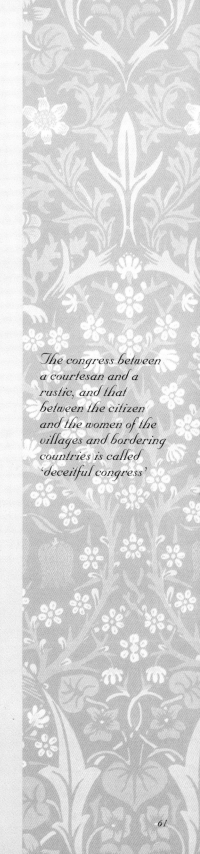

The congress between a courtesan and a rustic, and that between the citizen and the women of the villages and bordering countries is called 'deceitful congress'

When a woman stands on her hands and feet like a quadruped, and her lover mounts her like a bull, it is called the 'congress of a cow'. At this time everything that is ordinarily done on the bosom should be done on the back. In the same way can be carried on the congress of a dog, the congress of a goat, the congress of a deer, the forcible mounting of an ass, the congress of a cat, the jump of a tiger, the pressing of an elephant, the rubbing of a boar, and the mounting of a horse. And in all these cases the characteristics of these different animals should be manifested by acting like them.

When a man enjoys two women at the same time, both of whom love him equally, it is called the 'united congress'.

When a man enjoys many women altogether, it is called the 'congress of a herd of cows'. The following kinds of congress-sporting in water, or the congress of an elephant with many female elephants which is said to take place only in the water, the congress of a collection of goats, the congress of a collection of deer take place in imitation of these animals. In Gramaneri, many young men enjoy a woman that may be married to one of them, either one after the other, or at the same time. Thus one of them holds her, another enjoys her, a third uses her mouth, a fourth holds her middle part, and in this way they go on enjoying her several parts alternately. The same things can be done when several men are sitting in company with one courtesan, or when one courtesan is alone with many men. In the same way this can be done by the women of the king's harem when they accidentally get hold of a man. The people in the Southern countries have also a congress in the anus, that is called the 'lower congress'.

'An ingenious person should multiply the kinds of congress after the fashion of the different kinds of beasts and of birds. For these different kinds of congress, performed according to the usage of each country, and the liking of each individual, generate love, friendship, and respect in the hearts of women.'

LOVE BLOWS

Sexual intercourse can be compared to a quarrel, on account of the contrarieties of love and its tendency to dispute. The place of striking with passion is the body.

love making

When a woman lies down resting on a pillow or bed and opens her legs in the yawning position the men should give her support by holding her by the ankles and lower her yoni into his lingam in such a way that only the upper part of yoni remains in touch, this is also known as 'piercing'

Auparishtaka, or 'sucking the mango fruit' was practiced by eunuch, female attendants and female masseurs.
The carvings, seen on these pages adorn the walls of the Honarak Sun Temple in Orrisa, which dates back to the tenth century

Blows with the fist should be given on the back of the woman while she is sitting on the lap of the man, and she should give blows in return, abusing the man as if she were angry, and making the cooing and the weeping sounds. While the woman is engaged in congress the space between the breasts should be struck with the back of the hand, slowly at first, and then proportionately to the increasing excitement, until the end. When the man, making the sound Phât, strikes the woman on the head, with the fingers of his hand a little contracted, it is called Prasritaka, which means striking with the fingers of the hand a little contracted. In this case the appropriate sounds are the cooing sound and at the end of congress the sighing and weeping sounds.

At all times when kissing and such like things are begun, the woman should give a reply with a hissing sound. During the excitement when the woman is not accustomed to striking, she continually utters words expressive of prohibition, sufficiently, or desire of liberation, as well as the words 'father', 'mother',

love making

When the woman sees that her lover is tired of love making, she should cajole him to provide her oral pleasures at the same time giving him the same. Vatsyayana says that the things enjoyed by a man can also be enjoyed by the woman

intermingled with the sighing, weeping and thundering sounds. Towards the conclusion of the congress, the breasts, the jaghana, and the sides of the woman should be pressed with the open palms of the hand, with some force, until the end of it, and then sounds like those of the quail or the goose should be made.

'The characteristics of manhood are said to consist of roughness and impetuosity, while weakness, tenderness, sensibility, and an inclination to turn away from unpleasant things are the distinguishing marks of womanhood. The excitement of passion, and peculiarities of habit may sometimes cause contrary results to appear, but these do not last long, and in the end the natural state is resumed.'

The wedge on the bosom, the scissors on the head, the piercing instrument on the cheeks, and the pinchers on the breasts and sides, may also be taken into consideration with the other four modes of striking, and thus give eight ways altogether. But these four ways of striking with instruments are peculiar to the people of the southern countries, and the marks caused

love making

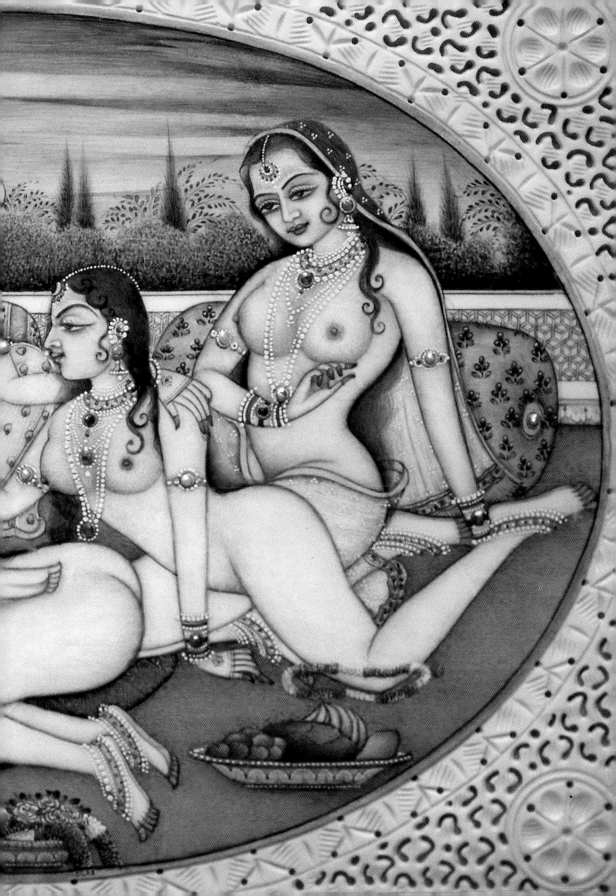

by them are seen on the breasts of their women. They are local peculiarities, but Vatsyayana is of opinion that the practice of them is painful, barbarous and base, and quite unworthy of imitation.

'Such passionate actions and amorous gesticulations or movements, which arise on the spur of the moment, and during sexual intercourse, cannot be defined, and are as irregular as dreams. A horse having once attained the fifth degree of motion goes on with blind speed, regardless of pits, ditches, and posts in his way; and in the same manner a loving pair become's blind with passion in the heat of congress, go on with great impetuosity, paying not the least regard to excess. For this reason one who is well acquainted with the science of love, and knowing his own strength, as also the tenderness, impetuosity, and strength of the young women, should act accordingly. The various modes of enjoyment are not for all times or for all persons, but they should only be used at the proper time and place.'

Men who are well acquainted with the art of love are well aware how often one woman differs from another in her sighs and sounds during the time of congress. Some women like to be talked to in the most loving way, others in the most lustful way, others in the most abusive way, and so on. Some women enjoy themselves with closed eyes in silence, others make a great noise over it, and some almost faint away. The great art is to ascertain what gives them the greatest pleasure.

ROLE REVERSAL (WOMAN ON TOP)

When a woman sees that her lover is fatigued by constant congress, without having his desire satisfied, she should lay him down upon his back, and give him assistance by acting his part. She may also do this to satisfy the curiosity of her lover, or her own desire of novelty.

There are two ways of doing this, the first is when during congress she turns round, and gets on the top of her lover, in such a manner as to continue the congress, without obstructing the pleasure of it; and the other is when she acts the man's part from the beginning. At such a time, with flowers in her hair hanging loose, and her smiles broken by hard breathings, she should

(facing page) life imitating art, or art imitating life

(Previous pages) When a man enjoys two women at the same time both of whom love him equally, it is called the 'united congress', but when a man enjoys many women at the same time, it is called congress of a 'herd of cows'

This is an artist's version of role reversal. The woman is sitting across the man's body opening her thighs and yoni in the Indrani position for man to reach deep inside her. She is playing on an musical instrument to have live music while making love.

press upon her lover's bosom with her own breasts, and lowering her head frequently, should do in return the same actions which he used to do before, returning his blows and chaffing him, should say, 'I was laid down by you, and fatigued with hard congress, I shall now therefore lay you down in return.' She should then again manifest her own bashfulness, her fatigue, and her desire of stopping the congress.

When a woman acts the part of a man, she has the following things to do:

When the woman holds the lingam in her yoni, draws it in, presses it, and keeps it thus in her for a long time, it is called the 'pair of tongs'. When, while engaged in congress, she turns round like a wheel, it is called the 'top'. This is learnt by practice only. When, on such an occasion, the man lifts up the middle

love making

During love making you can make out when a woman is closer to the orgasm, her body goes through spasms, breathing becomes harder, sweat breaks out making her body slippery, she cries out repeatedly egging her lover to go on and not stop.

part of his body, and the woman turns round her middle part, it is called the 'swing'. When the woman is tired, she should place her forehead on that of her lover, and should thus take rest without disturbing the union of the organs, and when the woman has rested herself the man should turn round and begin the congress again.

Whatever is done by a man for giving pleasure to a woman is called the work of a man, and is as follows:

While the woman is lying on his bed, and is as it were abstracted by his conversation, he should loosen the knot of her undergarments, and when she begins to dispute with him, he should overwhelm her with kisses. Then when his lingam is erect he should touch her with his hands in various places, and gently manipulate various parts of the body. If the woman is bashful,

love making

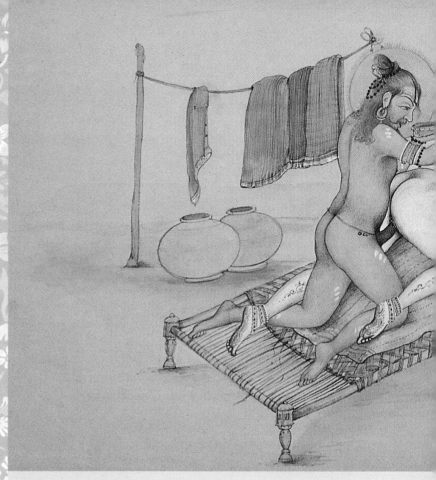

When the passion becomes intense one is advised to take on the position of various animals, such as a bull mounting a cow. The woman should kneel face down on her fours while her lover should mount her from the rear. At this time the things normally done with the breasts should be done on the back

and if it is the first time that they have come together, the man should place his hands between her thighs, which she would probably keep close together, and if she is a very young girl, he should first get his hands upon her breasts, which she would probably cover with her own hands, and under her armpits and on her neck. If however she is a seasoned woman, he should do whatever is agreeable either to him or to her, and whatever is fitting for the occasion. After this he should take hold of her hair, and hold her chin in his fingers for the purpose of kissing her. On this, if she is a young girl, she will become bashful and close her eyes. Anyhow, he should gather from the action of the woman what things would be pleasing to her during congress. While a man is doing to the woman what he likes best during congress, he should always make a point of pressing those parts of her body on which she turns her eyes and moans softly.

The signs of the enjoyment and satisfaction of the woman are as follows: her body relaxes, she closes her eyes, she puts aside

love making

all bashfulness, and shows increased willingness to unite the two organs as closely together as possible. On the other hand, the signs of her want of enjoyment and of failing to be satisfied are as follows: she shakes her hands, she does not let the man get up, feels dejected, bites the man, kicks him, and continues to go on moving after the man has finished. In such cases the man should rub the yoni of the woman with his hand and fingers (as the elephant rubs anything with his trunk) before engaging in congress, until it is softened and moist, after that is done he should proceed to put his lingam into her.

When the organs are brought together properly and directly it is called 'moving the organ forward'. When the lingam is held with the hand, and turned all round in the yoni, it is called 'churning'. When the yoni is lowered, and the upper part of it is struck with the lingam, it is called 'piercing'. When the same thing is done on the lower part of the yoni, it is called 'rubbing'. When the yoni is pressed by the lingam for a long time, it is called 'pressing'. When the lingam is removed to some distance from the yoni, and then forcibly strikes it, it is called 'giving a blow'. When only one part of the yoni is rubbed with the lingam, it is called the 'blow of a boar'. When both sides of the yoni are rubbed in this way, it is called the 'blow of a bull'. When the lingam is in the yoni, and moved up and down frequently, and without being taken out, it is called the 'sporting of a sparrow'. This takes place at the end of congress.

AUPARISHTAKA OR SUCKING A MANGO FRUIT

There are two kinds of eunuchs, those that are disguised as males and those that are disguised as females. Eunuchs disguised as females imitate their dress, speech, gestures, tenderness, timidity, simplicity, softness and bashfulness. The acts that are done on the jaghana or middle parts of women, are done in the mouths of these eunuchs, and this is called Auparishtaka. These eunuchs derive their imaginable pleasure, and their livelihood from this kind of congress, and they lead the life of courtesans.

Eunuchs disguised as males keep their desires secret, and when they wish to do anything they lead the life of masseurs. Under the pretence of massaging, a eunuch of this kind embraces and draws towards himself the thighs of the man whom he is massaging, and after this he touches the joints of his thighs and his jaghana, or central portions of his body. Then, if he finds the lingam of the man erect, he presses it with his hands and chaffs him for getting into that state. If after this, and after knowing his intention, the man does not tell the eunuch to proceed, then the latter does it of his own accord and begins the congress. If however he is ordered by the man to do it, then he disputes with him, and only consents at last with difficulty.

When, holding the man's lingam with his hand, and placing it between his lips, the eunuch moves about his mouth, it is called the 'nominal congress'. When, covering the end of the lingam with his fingers collected together like the bud of a plant or flower, the eunuch presses the sides of it with his lips, using his teeth also, it is called 'biting the sides'.

When, being desired to proceed, the eunuch presses the end

This position, as seen on the opposite page, can be improvised when the passion runs high, and the caution is thrown to the wind. Here the woman is turned upside down and her lover enters her yoni repeatedly, in small blows, to excite her passion. Practice makes the outcome of such position successful

love making

When the female raises both her thighs straight up it is called the 'rising position'. And when she raises both her legs and places them on her lover's shoulders, it is called the 'yawning position'

of the lingam with his lips closed together, and kisses it as if he were drawing it out, it is called the 'outside pressing'. When, being asked to go on, he puts the lingam further into his mouth, and presses it with his lips and then takes it out, it is called the 'inside pressing'. When, holding the lingam in his hand, the eunuch kisses it as if he were kissing the lower lip, it is called 'kissing'. When, after kissing it, he touches it with his tongue everywhere, and passes the tongue over the end of it, it is called 'rubbing'. When, in the same way, he puts the half of it into his mouth, and forcibly kisses and sucks it, this is called 'sucking a mango fruit'. And lastly, when, with the consent of the man, the eunuch puts the whole lingam into his mouth, and presses it to the very end, as if he were going to swallow it

l o v e   m a k i n g

up, it is called 'swallowing up'. It is ideal if all these can be done one after another. Striking, scratching, and other things may also be done during this kind of congress. The Auparishtaka is practised also by unchaste women, female attendants and serving maids, i.e. those who are not married to anybody, but who live by massaging.

The Acharyas or learned men, are of opinion that Auparishtaka is the work of a dog and not of a man, because it is a low practice, and opposed to the orders of the Holy Writ, and because the man himself suffers by bringing his lingam into contact with the mouths of eunuchs and women. Vatsyayana's opinion is that the orders of the Holy Writ do not affect those who resort to courtesans, and the law prohibits

After guiding the lingam in her yoni, the lady lifts her middle part and with her hands taking support of the ground, at this time she enjoys the love blows given by her lover

love making

the practice of the Auparishtaka with married women only. As regards the injury to the male, that can be easily remedied with herbs.

Auparishtaka, should not be abandoned on account of the interpretation of being un-clean according to some, because religious law, on the authority of which they are reckoned pure, lays down that the udder of a cow is clean at the time of milking, though the mouth of a cow, and also the mouth of her calf, are considered unclean by Hindus. Again a dog is clean when he seizes a deer in hunting, though food touched by a dog is otherwise considered very unclean. A bird is clean when it causes a fruit to fall from a tree by pecking at it, though things eaten by crows and other birds are considered unclean. The mouth of a woman is clean for kissing and such like things at the time of sexual intercourse. Vatsyayana thinks that in all things connected with love, everybody should act according to the custom of his country, and his own inclination and passion,

'The male servants of some men carry on the mouth congress with their masters. It is also practised by some citizens, who know each other well, among themselves. Some women of the harem, when they are amorous, do the acts of the mouth on the yonis of one another, and some men do the same thing with women. The way of doing this (i.e. of kissing the yoni) should be known from kissing the mouth. When a man and woman lie down in an inverted order, i.e. with the head of the one towards the feet of the other and carry on this congress, it is called the "congress of a crow".'

For the love of oral sex, courtesans abandon men possessed of good qualities and become attached to low persons, such as slaves and elephant drivers. The Auparishtaka, or mouth congress, should never be done by a learned Brahmin, by a minister, that carries on the business of a state, or by a man of good reputation, because though the practice is allowed by the Shastras (ancient texts), there is no reason why it should be carried on, and need only be practised in particular cases. The place, time and occasion to have oral sex should be carefully chosen. Because these things are done secretly, and the mind of the man being fickle, there is enormous amount of risk involved, especially from the person who is performing the act.

When the woman places one of her thighs across the thigh of her lover it is called the 'twining position'. When a woman forcibly holds in her Yoni the lingam after it is in, it is called the 'mare's position'

love making

Licking, biting, kissing and caressing should be done alternately during the act of love. No fixed order is to define as the heat of the moment decides their rhythm. here the lady is caressing her lover's lingam while he is seen licking her ankle

The practice of mouth congress appears to have been prevalent in ancient India. The Shustruta, a work on medicine some two thousand years old, describes the wounding of the lingam with the teeth as one of the causes of a disease treated upon in that work. Traces of the practice are found as far back as the eighth century, for various kinds of the Auparishtaka are represented in the sculptures of the temples at Bhubaneshwar, in Orissa, which were built around that period. It does not seem to be so prevalent now, its place perhaps being filled up by the practice of sodomy, introduced since the coming of the Muslims.

HOW TO BEGIN AND END

In the pleasure-room, decorated with flowers, and fragrant with perfumes, attended by his friends and servants, the citizen should receive the woman, who will come bathed and dressed,

Passion has no fixed place or time as shown in this miniature painting. Lovers are taking advantage of the cover of darkness and making love in the shadow of the stars. The urgency of the occasion can be seen as they still have their clothes on

and will invite her to take refreshment and to drink freely. He should then seat her on his left side, and holding her hair, and touching also the end and knot of her garment, he should gently embrace her with his right arm. They should then carry on an amusing conversation on various subjects, and may also talk suggestively of things not to be mentioned generally in society. They may then sing, either with or without gesticulations, and play musical instruments, talk about the arts, and persuade each other to drink. At last when the woman is overcome with love and desire, the man should dismiss the people that may be with him, giving them flowers, ointments, and betel leaves, and then when the two are left alone, they should proceed as has been already described in the previous chapters.

At the end of the congress, the lovers with modesty, and not looking at each other, should go separately to the washing-room.

After this, they should eat some betel leaves, and the man should apply sandalwood or other fragrant ointment on the breasts of the woman. He should then embrace her with his left arm, and should coax her to drink from a cup held in his own hand. They can then eat sweetmeats, according to their likings and may drink fresh juice, extracts of meat, sherbet, the juice of mango fruits, the extract of the juice of the citron tree mixed with sugar, or anything that may be liked in different countries, and known to be sweet, soft, and pure. The lovers may also sit on the terrace of the palace or house, and enjoy the moonlight, and carry on an agreeable conversation. While the woman lies in his lap, with her face towards the moon, the man should show her the different planets, the morning star, the polar star, and the seven Rishis, or Great Bear.

KINDS OF CONGRESS

When a man and a woman, who love each other, come together with great difficulty, or when one of the two returns from a journey, or is reconciled after having been separated on account of a quarrel, then congress is called the 'loving congress'. It is carried on according to the liking of the lovers, and as long as they choose. When two persons come together, while their love for each other is still in its infancy, their congress is called the 'congress of subsequent love'.

When a man carries on the congress by exciting himself by means of the sixty-four ways, such as kissing, biting etc. or when a man and a woman come together, though in reality they are both attached to different persons, their congress is then called 'congress of artificial love'. At this time all the ways and means mentioned in the Kama Shastra should be used. When a man, from the beginning to the end of the congress, though having connection with the woman, thinks all the time that he is enjoying another one whom he desires, it is called the 'congress of transferred love'.

Congress between a man and a female water carrier, or a female servant of a caste lower than his own, lasting only until the desire is satisfied, is called 'congress like that of eunuchs'. Here external touches, kisses, and manipulation are not to be

love making

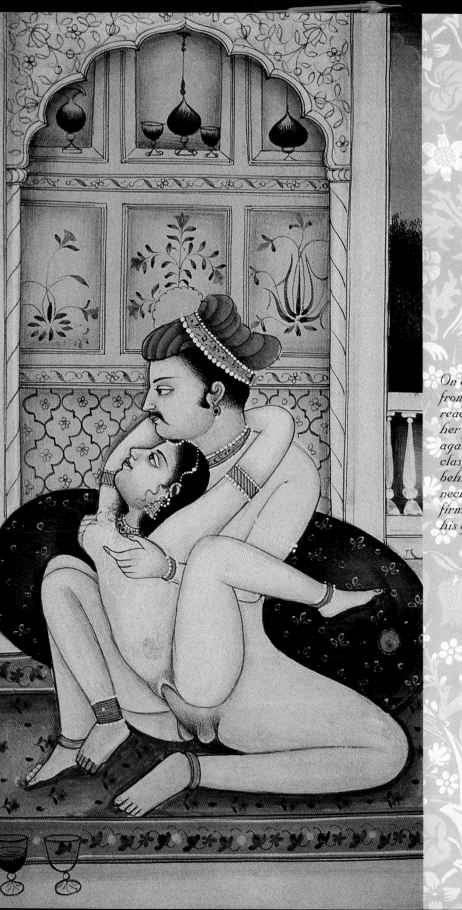

On entering her
from behind, a lover
reaches new depths of
her yoni; she sits up
against his chest and
clasps her arms
behind her lover's
neck. This leaves her
firm breasts within
his grasp

employed. The congress between a courtesan and a rustic, and that between citizens and the women of villages, and bordering countries, is called 'deceitful congress'. The congress that takes place between two persons who are attached to one another, and which is done according to their own liking is called 'spontaneous congress'.

LOVE QUARRELS

A woman who is very much in love with a man cannot bear to hear the name of her rival mentioned, or be addressed by her name by mistake. If this happens, a great quarrel arises, and the woman cries, becomes angry, tosses her hair about, strikes her lover, falls from her bed or seat, and, casting aside her garlands and ornaments, throws herself down on the ground. At this time, the lover should attempt to reconcile her with conciliatory words. But she, not replying to his questions, and with increased anger, should bend down his head by pulling his hair, and having kicked him once, twice, or thrice on his arms, head, bosom or back, should then proceed to the door of the room. Dattaka says that she should then sit angrily near the door and shed tears, but should not go out, because she would be found fault with for going away. After a time, when she thinks that the conciliatory words and actions of her lover have reached their utmost, she should then embrace him, talking to him with harsh and reproachful words, but at the same time showing a loving desire for congress.

When the woman is in her own house, and has quarreled with her lover, she should go to him and show how angry she is, and leave him. Afterwards the man should sent his emissaries to pacify her. She should return to the house, with them and spend the night with her lover.

A man, employing the sixty-four means mentioned in Kamasutra, enjoys the woman of the first quality. Though he may speak well on other subjects, if he does not know the sixty-four arts of Kamasutra, no great respect is paid to him in the assembly of the learned. A man skilled in the sixty-four arts is looked upon with love by his own wife, by the wives of others, and by courtesans.

When a man and a woman support themselves on each others bodies and make love while standing, it is called the 'supported congress'. In the painting a child is seen wanting woman's attention while man is pulling her closer for a tighter embrace and avoiding distraction

'Though a woman is reserved, and keeps her feelings concealed;
yet when she gets on the top of a man, she then shows all her love and desire.
A man should gather from the actions of the woman of what disposition she is,
and in what way she likes to be enjoyed.
A woman during her monthly courses, a woman who has been lately confined,
and a fat woman should not be made to act the part of a man.'

courtship

While choosing a girl
one should make sure
that she is younger
than you by at least
four years, her body
should be supple and
free from blemishes
and her breast firm
and upright.
Her parents should
be wealthy and
command good
position in the society

hen a virgin girl of the same caste is married in accordance with the precepts of Holy Writ, the results of such a union are the acquisition of Dharma and Artha. Children, affinity, increase of friends, and untarnished love are characteristics of such union. For this reason a man should choose a girl who is of good family, whose parents are alive, and who is three years or more younger than himself. She should be born of a highly respectable family, possessed of wealth, well connected, and with many relations and friends. She should also be beautiful, of a good disposition, with lucky marks on her body, and with good hair, nails, teeth, ears, eyes and firm breasts. The man should, of course, also possess these qualities himself. But at all events, a girl who is not a virgin should never be loved, for it would be reproachable to do such a thing.

In order to marry a girl as described above, the parents and relations of the man should exert themselves. The friends of the boy should bring to the notice of the girl's parents, the faults of other prospective grooms and should at the same time exaggerate all the qualities of their friend, particularly those that may be admired by the girl's mother. One of the friends should also disguise himself as an astrologer, and declare the good fortune and wealth of his friend by showing the existence of all the lucky omens (flight of a blue jay on persons left is considered a lucky omen), the good influence of planets, the auspicious entrance of the sun into a sign of the Zodiac, and fortunate marks on his body. Others again should rouse the jealousy of the girl's mother by telling her that their friend is getting offers from some other quarter of even a better girl than her daughter.

A girl should be taken as a wife, as also given in marriage, when fortune, signs, omens, and the words of others are favourable. A man should not marry a girl who is asleep, crying, or gone out of the house when sought in marriage, or who is betrothed to another.

The following kinds of prospective brides should be avoided: the one who is kept concealed, one who has an ill-sounding name, one who has her nostril turned up, one who is formed like a male, one who has crooked thighs, one who has a projecting forehead, one who has a bald head, one who does not like purity, one who has

been polluted by another, one who is affected with the glandular disease, one who is disfigured in any way, one who has fully arrived at puberty, one who has sweaty hands and feet.

In the same way a girl who is called by the name of one of the twenty-seven stars, or by the name of a tree, or of a river, and also a girl whose name ends in 'r' or 'l' is considered worthless. It is said that prosperity is gained only by marrying that girl to whom one becomes attached, and therefore no other girl should be married except the one who is loved by you.

When a girl comes of marriageable age, her parents should dress her smartly, and take her to places where everyone can see her. Every afternoon, they should send her with her female companions to sports, sacrifices, and marriage ceremonies, and thus show her to society, because she is a kind of merchandise. They should also welcome any prospective bridegroom and wait for an invitation from his parents.

When a girl is thus acquired, either according to the custom of the country or according to his own desire, the man should marry her in accordance with the precepts of the Holy Writ, according to one of the four kinds of marriage.

'Amusement in society, such as completing verses begun by others, marriages, and auspicious ceremonies should be carried on neither with superiors, nor inferiors, but with our equals. That should be known as a high connection when a man, after marrying a girl, has to serve her and her relations afterwards like a servant, and such a connection is censured by the good. On the other hand, that reproachable connection, where a man, together with his relations, lords it over his wife, is called a low connection by the wise. But when both the man and the woman afford mutual pleasure to each other, and when the relatives on both sides pay respect to one another, such is called a connection in the proper sense of the word. Therefore a man should contract neither a high connection by which he is obliged to bow down afterwards to his kinsmen, nor a low connection, which is universally reprehended by all.'

SEDUCING OR INITIATING THE FIRST MOVE

For the first three days after marriage, the girl and her husband should sleep on the floor, abstain from sexual pleasures, and eat

In this rare painting one can see a Maharaja and his whole entourage of concubines playing with colours during the festival of Holi. There is a customary drink called bhang made out of the cannabis plant, which is served in liberal doses during the festival, it is an exhilarating experience to apply colour on people and get coloured during the festival

A South Indian wall fresco shows a Hindu god with his consort in a jungle surrounded by wild animals who are also seem to be caught in sensual ecstasy

their food without seasoning it either with alkali or salt. For the next seven days they should bathe amidst the sounds of auspicious musical instruments, should decorate themselves, dine together, and pay attention to their relations as well as to those who may have come to witness their marriage. This is applicable to persons of all castes. On the night of the tenth day the man should begin in a lonely place with soft words, and thus create confidence in the girl.

Some authors say that for the purpose of winning her over he should not speak to her for three days, but the followers of Babhravya are of opinion that if the man does not speak with her for three days, the girl may be discouraged by seeing him spiritless like a pillar, and she may begin to despise him as a eunuch. Vatsyayana says that the man should begin to win her over, and to create confidence in her, but should abstain at first from sexual

courtship

A Tantrik Buddhist
fresco from the
Himalayan region
depicts the union of
male and female
energies in a
meditative pose

pleasures. Women, being of a tender nature, want tender begin-
nings, and when they are forcibly approached by men with whom
they are but slightly acquainted, they sometimes suddenly become
haters of sexual connection, and sometimes even haters of the
male sex. The man should therefore approach the girl according to
her liking, and should make use of those devices by which he may
be able to establish himself more and more into her confidence.
These devices are as follows:

He should embrace her first of all in a way she likes most,
because it does not last for a long time. He should embrace her
with the upper part of his body because that is easier and simpler.
If the girl is grown up, or if the man has known her for some time,
he may embrace her by the light of a lamp, but if he is not well
acquainted with her, or if she is a young girl, he should then

courtship

This eighth century sculpture from Ellora Cave Temple shows a woman reaching out for her lover by putting her arms around his neck and pulling his face towards her for a passionate kiss, man in the meanwhile excites her even more by cupping and playing with her breasts

embrace her in darkness. When the girl accepts the embrace, the man should put a tambula or screw of betel nut and betel leaves in her mouth, and if she will not take it, he should induce her to do so by conciliatory words, entreaties, oaths, and kneeling at her feet, for it is a universal rule that however bashful or angry a woman may be she never disregards a man's kneeling at her feet. At the time of giving this tambula he should trace his fingers on her lips and kiss her mouth softly and gracefully without making any sound. When she is gained over in this respect he should then make her talk, and he should ask her questions about things of which he knows or pretends to know nothing, and which can be answered in a few words. If she does not speak to him, he should not frighten her, but should ask her the same thing again and again in a conciliatory manner. If she does not then speak he should urge her to give a reply because, as Ghotakamukha says, 'all girls hear everything said to them by men, but do not themselves sometimes say a single word'.

When she gains confidence, the girl should give replies by shakes of the head, but if she has quarreled with the man she should not even do that. When she is asked by the man whether she likes him, she should remain silent for a long time, and when at last forced to reply, should give him a favourable answer by a nod of her head. If the man is previously acquainted with the girl he should converse with her by means of a female friend, who may be in the confidence of both. On such an occasion the girl should smile with her head bent down, and if the female friend say more on her part than she was desired to do, she should chide her and dispute with her. The female friend should say in jest even what she is not desired to say by the girl, and add, 'she says so', on which the girl should say indistinctly and prettily, 'O no! I did not say so', and she should then smile and throw an occasional glance towards the man.

If the girl is familiar with the man, she should place near him, without saying anything, the tambula, the ointment, or the garland that he may have asked for, or she may tie them up in his upper garment. While she is engaged in this, the man should touch her young breasts in the sounding way of pressing with the nails, and if she prevents him doing this he should say to her, 'I will not do it again if you will embrace me', and should in this way cause her to embrace him. While he is being embraced by her, he should pass

his hand repeatedly over her body. Eventually he should place her in his lap, and try to gain her consent, and if she will not yield to him he should frighten her by saying 'I shall impress marks of my teeth and nails on your lips and breasts, and then make similar marks on my own body, and shall tell my friends that you did them. What will you say then?' In this and other ways, as fear and confidence are created in the minds of children, so should the man gain her over to his wishes.

On the second and third nights, after her confidence has increased still more, he should feel the whole of her body with his hands, and kiss her all over; he should also place his hands upon her thighs and rub them softly, and if he succeed in this he should then massage the joints of her thighs. If she tries to prevent him doing this he should say to her, 'What harm is there in doing it?' and should persuade her to let him do it. After gaining this point he should touch her private parts, should loosen her girdle and the knot of her dress, and turning up her lower garment should massage the joints of her naked thighs. Under various pretences he should do all these things, but he should not at that time begin actual congress.

Passionate men are always thinking of making love either to their respective wives, concubines and female attendants

courtship

For a virgin who is shy, her confidence can be gained by luring her to a lonely place, there after one should proceed by caressing and petting different parts of her body in order to subside her shyness. In this painting the man is sitting on his haunches along with the woman and is rubbing her yoni and breasts in order to excite her passion

'A man acting according to the inclinations of a girl should try to gain her over
so that she may love him and place her confidence in him.
A man does not succeed either by implicitly following the inclination of a girl,
or by wholly opposing her, and he should therefore adopt a middle course.
He who knows how to make himself loved by women,
as well as to increase their honour and create confidence in them,
becomes an object of their love.
But he who neglects a girl, thinking she is too bashful,
is despised by her as a beast ignorant of the working of the female mind.
Moreover, a girl forcibly enjoyed by one who does not understand the hearts
of girls becomes nervous, uneasy, and dejected,
and suddenly begins to hate the man who has taken advantage of her;
and then, when her love is not understood or returned,
she sinks into despondency, and becomes either a hater of mankind altogether,
or, hating her own man, she has recourse to other men.'

marriage

On marriage, care
should be taken that
the passion is
distributed equally
among various wives.
It is responsibility of
the eldest wife to teach
the younger ones how
to impart maximum
pleasure to the
husband

hen a man has thus begun to woo the girl he
loves, he should spend his time with her and
amuse her with various games and diversions appropriate for their age, such as pick-
ing and collecting flowers, making garlands
of flowers, playing the parts of members of a
fictitious family, cooking food, playing with dice, playing with cards,
the game of odd and even, the game of finding out the middle finger, the game of six pebbles, and such other games as may be in
vogue, and be sensitive to the mood swings of the girl.

In addition to this, he should carry on various amusing games
played by several persons together, such as hide and seek, playing
with seeds, hiding things in several small heaps of wheat and
looking for them, blind man's buff, gymnastic exercises, and other
games of the same sort, in company with the girl, her friends
and female attendants.

The man should also show great kindness to any woman whom
the girl thinks fit to be trusted. Most importantly, he should attach to
himself by kindness daughter of the girl's nurse, for if she be gained
over, she will not cause any obstruction, but at times is able to effect
a union between him and the girl. And though she knows the true
character of the man, she always talks of his many excellent qualities to the parents and relations of the girl, even though she may not
be desired to do so by him.

In this way the man should do whatever the girl takes most pleasure in, and he should get for her whatever she desires to possess.
Things should be given at different times whenever he gets an
opportunity of meeting her. In short, he should try in every way to
make her look upon him as one who would do for her everything
that she wanted to be done.

He should get her to meet him privately, and should then tell her
that the reason of his giving presents to her in secret was the fear
that the parents of both of them might be displeased, and then he
may add that the things which he had given her had been much
desired by other people. When her love begins to show signs of
increasing, he should relate to her agreeable stories if she expresses
a wish to hear such narratives or if she takes delight in tricks,
he should amaze her by performing various tricks of jugglery; or if
she feels a great curiosity to see a performance of the various arts,

he should show his own skill in them. In short he should try to fill all her whims and fancies.

He should also teach the daughter of the girl's nurse all the sixty-four means of pleasure practised by men, and under this pretext should also inform her of his great skill in the art of sexual enjoyment. All this time he should wear a fine dress, and make as good an appearance as possible, for young women love men who are handsome, good looking and well dressed.

A girl always shows her love by outward signs and actions. She never looks at the man in the face, and becomes abashed when she is looked at by him; under some pretext or other she shows her limbs to him; she looks secretly at him though he has gone away from her side, hangs down her head when she is asked some question by him, and answers in indistinct words and unfinished sentences, delights to be in his company for a long time speaks to her attendants in a peculiar tone with the hope of attracting his attention towards her when she is at a distance from him, does not wish to go from the place where he is, under some pretext or other she makes him look at different things. She tells him tales and stories very slowly so that she may continue conversing with him for a long time, kisses and embraces before him a child sitting in her lap, draws ornamental marks on the foreheads of her female servants, performs sportive and graceful movements when her attendants speak jestingly to her in the presence of her lover. She even confides in her lover's friends, and respects and obeys them, shows kindness to his servants, converses with them, and engages them to do her work as if she were their mistress, and listens attentively to them when they tell stories about her lover to somebody else.

'A man, who has seen and perceived the feelings of the girl towards him, and who has noticed the outward signs and movements by which those feelings are expressed, should do everything in his power to seduce her. He should gain over the confidence of a young girl by childlike sports, a damsel come of age by his skill in the arts, and a girl that loves him by having recourse to persons in whom she confides.'

ABOUT THINGS TO BE DONE BY THE MAN AND WOMAN

When engaged with her in any game or sport he should inten-

In India, monsoon clouds and rain have been associated with love and romance. In this beautiful miniature painting one can see a prince, on the terrace of his palace, showing his beloved the swirling rain clouds in order to excite her passion. In the windows below a lady getting ready probably to join them on the terrace while the other one is feeding the fish in the pond

marriage

Konarak temple, in east India, near the city of Bhubaneshwar is decorated with the sculptures of asaras or the dancers of the heaven whose job was to entertain gods

tionally hold her hand. He should show her a pair of human beings cut out of the leaf of a tree, and such like things, at intervals. When swimming, he should dive at a distance from her, and come close to her. He should embrace her in different ways to make her feel that she is wanted by him all the time. He should relate to her the beautiful dream that he has had with reference to other women. At parties and assemblies he should sit near her, and touch her under some pretence or other, and having placed his foot upon hers, he should slowly touch each of her toes, and press the ends of the nails; if successful in this, he should get hold of her foot with his hand and repeat the same thing.

Whenever he sits with her on the same seat he should say to her, 'I have something to tell you in private', and then, when she comes

marriage

This figure of a voluptuous apsara is seen in Khajuraho temples in central India. The curves of her body accentuate the sensuousness her dasis or the attendants can be see on her either side

to hear it in a quiet place, he should express his love to her more by manner and signs than by words. When he comes to know the state of her feelings towards him he should pretend to be ill, and should make her come to his house to speak to him. He should come close to her by word and touch. When she wants to go away he should let her go, with an earnest request to come and see him again. This device of illness should be continued for three days and three nights. After this, when she begins coming to see him frequently, he should carry on long conversations with her, for, says Ghotakamukha, 'though a man loves a girl, he never succeeds in winning her without a great deal of talking'. At last, when the man finds the girl completely gained over, he may then begin to enjoy her. As for the saying that women grow less timid than usual during

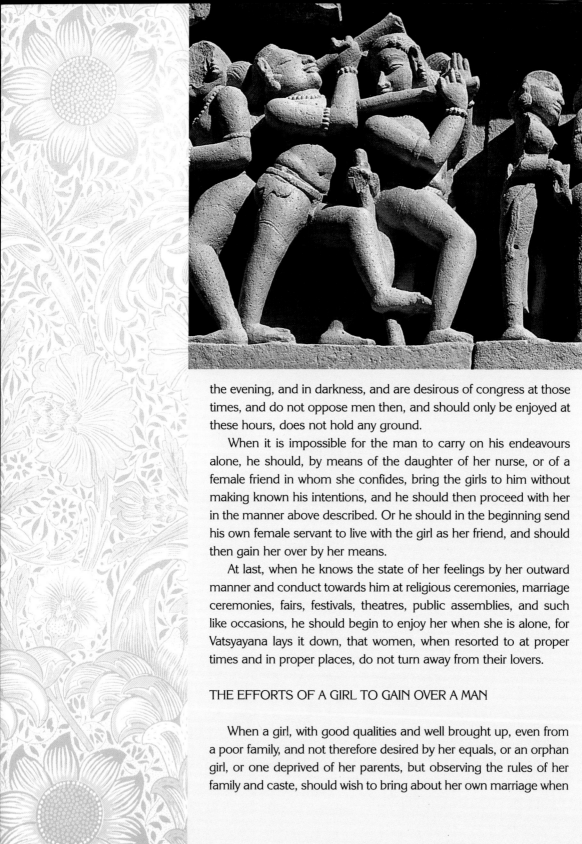

the evening, and in darkness, and are desirous of congress at those times, and do not oppose men then, and should only be enjoyed at these hours, does not hold any ground.

When it is impossible for the man to carry on his endeavours alone, he should, by means of the daughter of her nurse, or of a female friend in whom she confides, bring the girls to him without making known his intentions, and he should then proceed with her in the manner above described. Or he should in the beginning send his own female servant to live with the girl as her friend, and should then gain her over by her means.

At last, when he knows the state of her feelings by her outward manner and conduct towards him at religious ceremonies, marriage ceremonies, fairs, festivals, theatres, public assemblies, and such like occasions, he should begin to enjoy her when she is alone, for Vatsyayana lays it down, that women, when resorted to at proper times and in proper places, do not turn away from their lovers.

THE EFFORTS OF A GIRL TO GAIN OVER A MAN

When a girl, with good qualities and well brought up, even from a poor family, and not therefore desired by her equals, or an orphan girl, or one deprived of her parents, but observing the rules of her family and caste, should wish to bring about her own marriage when

she comes of age, such a girl should endeavour to win a strong and good looking young man, or a person whom she thinks would marry her on account of the weakness of his mind, and even without the consent of his parents. She should do this by such means as would endear her to the man, as well as by frequently seeing and meeting him. Her mother also should constantly cause them to meet by means of her female friends, and the daughter of her nurse. The girl herself should try to get alone with her beloved in some quiet place, and at odd times should give him flowers, betel nut, betel leaves and perfumes. She should also show her skill in the practice of the arts, in massaging, in scratching and in pressing with the nails. She should also talk to him on the subjects he likes best, and discuss with him the ways and means of gaining over and winning the affections of a girl.

Some authors say that although the girl loves the man, she should not offer herself, or make the first overtures, for a girl who does this loses her dignity, and is liable to be scorned and rejected. But when the man shows his wish to enjoy her, she should be favourable to him and should show no change in her demeanour when he embraces her, and should receive all the manifestations of his love as if she were ignorant of the state of his mind. But when he tries to kiss her she should oppose him; when he begs to be allowed to have sexual intercourse with her she should let him touch

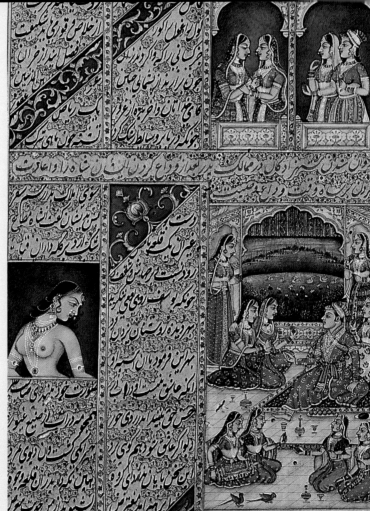

If one's beloved is getting married to someone else, on such occasion the man should not loose his heart but take the initiative to poison the girl's mother's mind against the prospective groom. If he is successful in doing so then he should invite the girl and her mother to the neighbour's house and get married there

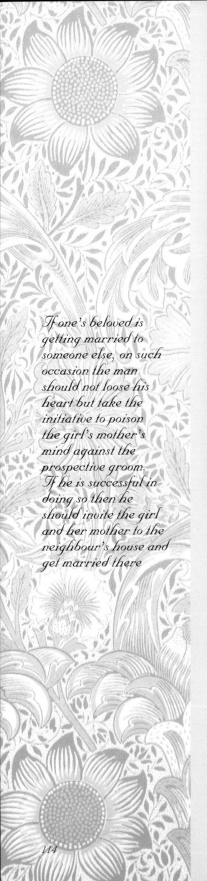

her private parts only and with considerable difficulty; and though propositioned by him repeatedly she should not yield herself up to him as if of her own accord, but should resist his attempts to have her. It is only, when she is certain that she is truly loved, and that her lover is indeed devoted to her, and will not change his mind, that she should then give herself up to him, and persuade him to marry her quickly. After losing her virginity she should tell her confidential friends about it.

'A girl who is much sought after should marry the man that she likes, and whom she thinks would be obedient to her, and capable of giving her pleasure. But when from the desire of wealth a girl is married by her parents to a rich man without taking into consideration the character or looks of the bridegroom, or when given to a man who has several wives, she never becomes attached to the man, even though he be endowed with good qualities, obedient to her will,

active, strong, and healthy, and anxious to please her in every way.

A husband who is obedient but yet master of himself, though he be poor and not good looking, is better than one who is common to many women, even though he be handsome and attractive. The wives of rich men, where there are many wives, are not generally attached to their husbands, and are not confidential with them, and even though they possess all the external enjoyments of life, still have recourse to other men. A man who is of a low mind, who has fallen from his social position, and who is much given to travelling, does not deserve to be married; neither does one who has many wives and children, or one who is devoted to sport and gambling, and who comes to his wife only when he likes. Of all the lovers of a girl he only is her true husband who possesses the qualities that are liked by her, and such a husband only enjoys real superiority over her, because he is the husband of love.'

marriage

DIFFERENT KINDS OF MARRIAGE

When a girl cannot meet her lover frequently in private, she should send the daughter of her nurse to him, that is, if she has confidence in her. On seeing the man, the daughter of the nurse should, in the course of conversation, describe to him the noble birth, the good disposition, the beauty, talent, skill, knowledge of human nature and affection of the girl in such a way as not to let him suppose that she had been sent by the girl, and should thus create affection for the girl in the heart of the man. To the girl also she should speak about the excellent qualities of the man, especially of those qualities which she knows are pleasing to the girl.

She should, moreover criticize the other lovers of the girl, and talk about the greediness and indiscretion of their parents, and the fickleness of their relations. She should also quote samples of many girls of ancient times, such as Shakuntala and others, who, having united themselves with lovers of their own caste and their own choice, were ever happy afterwards in their society. And she should

marriage

When the wife wants to approach her husband in private, her dress should consist of many ornaments, various kinds of flowers and on her body she should adorn sweet smelling ointments so that he may want to hold her very close and not let her go

also tell of other girls who married into great families, and being troubled by rival wives, became wretched and miserable, and were finally abandoned. She should further speak of the good fortune, the continual happiness, the chastity, obedience, and affection of the man, and if the girl gets amorous about him, she should endeavour to allay her shame and her fear as well as her suspicions about any disaster that might result from her marriage. In a word, she should act the whole part of a female messenger by telling the girl all about the man's affection for her, the places he frequented, and the endeavours he made to meet her, and by frequently repeating, 'It will be all right if the man will take you away forcibly and unexpectedly.'

THE FORMS OF MARRIAGE

After a man has chosen his bride and she also accepts him as her husband then he should perform the ritual to sanctify the marriage. He should spread the Kusha grass on the ground where he should build a holy fire, from the fire brought from the house of

marriage

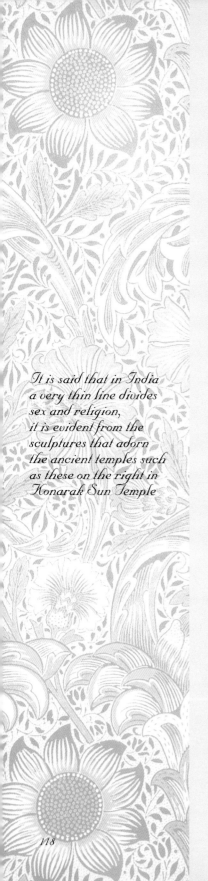

It is said that in India a very thin line divides sex and religion, it is evident from the sculptures that adorn the ancient temples such as these on the right in Konarak Sun Temple

a Brahmin. Then he should marry her according to the precepts of the religious law. After this he should inform his parents of the fact, because it is the opinion of ancient authors that a marriage solemnly contracted in the presence of fire cannot afterwards be set aside.

After the consummation of the marriage, the relations of the man should gradually be made acquainted with the affair, and the relations of the girl should also be apprised of it in such a way that they may consent to the marriage, and overlook the secret manner in which it was brought about, and when this is done they should afterwards be reconciled by affectionate presents and favourable conduct. In this manner the man should marry the girl according to the Gandharva form of marriage.

When the girl cannot make up her mind, or will not express her readiness to marry, the man should obtain her in any one of the following ways:

On a fitting occasion, and under some excuse, he should, by means of a female friend with whom he is well acquainted, and whom he can trust, and who also is well known to the girl's family, get the girl brought unexpectedly to his house, and he should then bring fire from the house of a Brahmin and marry her.

If the loved one is getting married to someone else, then in such calamity the man should poison the mind of the girl's mother against the future husband. Then on some pretext he should invite the mother and daughter, to a neighbour's house and get married, with their consent, in front of the fire brought from the house of the Brahmin.

The man should become a great friend of the brother of the girl, the said brother being of the same age as himself, and addicted to courtesans, and to intrigues with the wives of other people, and should give him assistance in such matters, and also give him occasional presents. He should then tell him about his great love for his sister, as young men will sacrifice even their lives for the sake of those who may be of the same age, habits, and dispositions as themselves. After this the man should get the girl brought by means of her brother to some secure place, and having brought fire from the house of a Brahmin should proceed as before.

The man should on the occasion of festivals get the daughter of the nurse to give the girl some intoxicating substance, and then cause her to be brought to some secure place under the pretence

m a r r i a g e

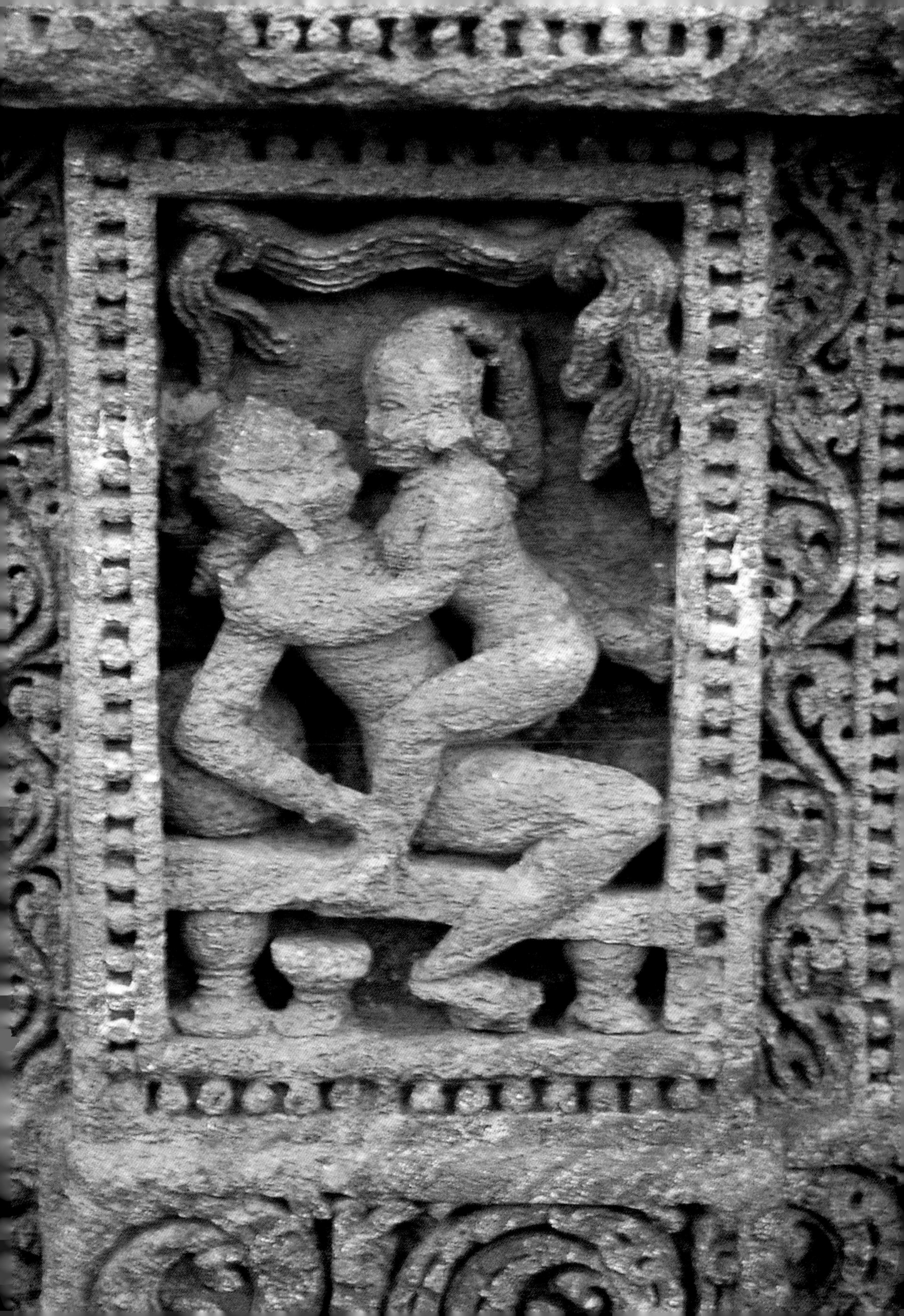

of some business, and there having enjoyed her before she recovers from her intoxication, should bring fire from the house of a Brahmin, and proceed as before.

The man should, with the connivance of the daughter of the nurse, carry off the girl from her house while she is asleep, and then, having enjoyed her before she recovers from her sleep, should bring fire from the house of a Brahmin, and proceed as before.

When the girl goes to a garden, or to some village in the neighbourhood, the man should, with his friends, fall on her guards, and having killed them, or frightened them away, forcibly carry her off, and proceed as before.

'In all the forms of marriage given in this chapter of this work, the one that precedes is better than the one that follows it on account of its being more in accordance with the commands of religion, and therefore it is only when it is impossible to carry the former into practice that the latter should be resorted to. As the fruit of all good marriages is love, the Gandharva form of marriage is respected, even though it is formed under unfavourable circumstances, because it fulfils the object sought for. Another cause of the respect accorded to the Gandharva form of marriage is that it brings forth happiness, causes less trouble in its performance than the other forms of marriage, and is above all the result of previous love.'

THE MANNER OF LIVING OF A VIRTUOUS WOMAN

A virtuous woman, who has affection for her husband, should act in conformity with his wishes as if he were a divine being, and with his consent should take upon herself the whole care of his family. She should keep the whole house well cleaned, and arrange flowers of various kinds in different parts of it, and make the floor smooth and polished so as to give the whole house a neat and becoming appearance. She should surround the house with a garden, and place all the materials required for the morning, noon and evening sacrifices. Moreover, she should herself revere the sanctuary of the Household Gods, for, says Gonardiya, 'nothing so much attracts the heart of a householder to his wife as a careful observance of the things mentioned above'.

Towards the parents, relations, friends, sisters, and servants of her husband she should behave as they deserve. In the garden

In India marriages have always been an elaborate affair, people spend more than they can afford to on such occasions. Here a groom can be seen riding on a white horse and is touching the toran at the entrance of the bride's house with his sword. Fireworks are going on in the background to mark the festivity

she should plant beds of green vegetables. Clusters of various flowers such as the jasmine, the yellow amaranth, the wild jasmine, the china rose and others, should likewise be planted, together with the fragrant grass. She should also have seats and arbours made in the garden, in the middle of which a pool should be dug.

The wife should always avoid the company of female beggars, female Buddhist mendicants, unchaste and roguish women, female fortune tellers and witches. As regards meals she should always consider what her husband likes and dislikes and what things are good for him, and what are injurious to him.

In the event of any misconduct on the part of her husband, she should not blame him excessively, though she should express her disappointment. She should not abuse him, but rebuke him. Moreover, she should not nag him, for, says Gonardiya, 'there is no cause of dislike on the part of a husband so great as this character-

marriage

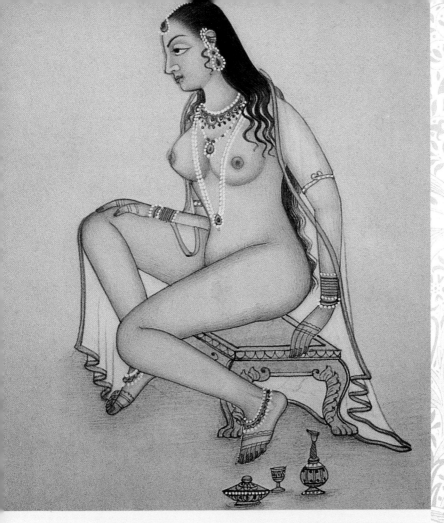

In a pleasure room,
decorated with
flowers, and fragrant
with perfumes man
should receive the
woman who will come
bathed and dressed
in thin muslin clothes.
He should then invite
her to sit with him and
lavish drinks on her

(Facing page) After
the marriage newly
wedded bride should
be approached with
regard and sensitivity.
If the husband is
forceful and
aggressive, she may
take dislike to him
and not allow him to
come near her at all

istic in a wife'. She should carry on day after day with a harassed look on her face.

When the wife wants to approach her husband in private her dress should consist of many ornaments, various kinds of flowers, and a cloth decorated with different colours, and some sweet-smelling ointments or unguents. But her everyday dress should be composed of a thin, close-textured cloth, a few ornaments and flowers, and a little scent, not too much. She should also observe the fasts and vows of her husband, and when he tries to prevent her doing this, she should persuade him to let her do it.

At appropriate times of the year, she should buy household provisions like earth, bamboos, firewood, skins, and iron pots, and also salt and oil. Fragrant substances, vessels made of the fruit of the plant, medicines, and other things should be obtained when required and kept in a secret place of the house. The seeds of

marriage

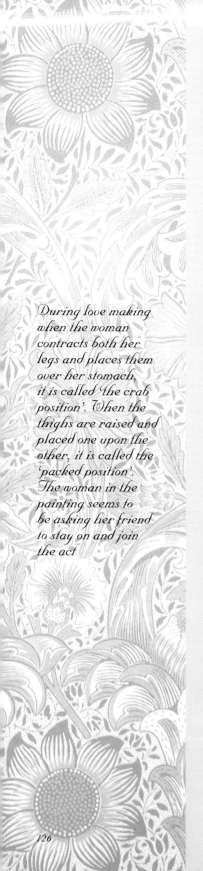

During love making when the woman contracts both her legs and places them over her stomach, it is called 'the crab position'. When the thighs are raised and placed one upon the other, it is called the 'packed position'. The woman in the painting seems to be asking her friend to stay on and join the act

vegetables, should be bought and sown at the proper seasons.

The wife, moreover, should never tell to strangers the amount of her wealth, nor the secrets which her husband has confided to her. She should be very careful with expenditure and stick to the household budget.

She should reward the servants by giving them gifts or things that are no longer required in the household. Some provisions like utensils should be carefully presented. For instance the vessels in which wine is prepared, as well as those in which it is kept, should be carefully looked after, and put away at the proper time. All sales and purchases should also be well attended to. The friends of her husband she should welcome by presenting them with flowers, ointment, incense, betel leaves, and betel nut. She should treat her in laws as they deserve, always remaining dependent on their will, never contradicting them, speaking to them in few and not harsh words, not laughing loudly in their presence, and acting with their friends and enemies as with her own. In addition to the above she should not be vain, or too much taken up with her enjoyments. She should be liberal towards her servants, and reward them on holidays and festivals; and not give away anything without first making it known to her husband.

THE BEHAVIOUR OF A WIFE DURING THE ABSENCE OF HER HUSBAND ON A JOURNEY

During the absence of her husband on a journey, the virtuous woman should wear only her auspicious ornaments, and observe the fasts in honour of the Gods. While anxious to hear the news of her husband, she should still look after her household affairs. She should sleep near the elder women of the house, and be pleasant to them. She should look after all the things that are liked by her husband, and continue the works that have been begun by him. She should not go to her relations except on occasions of joy and sorrow. The fasts and feasts should be observed with the consent of the elders of the house. And when her husband returns from his journey, she should receive him at first in her ordinary clothes, so that he may know in what way she has lived during his absence, and should bring to him some presents, as also materials for the worship of the Deity.

marriage

'The wife, whether she be a woman of noble family, or a virgin widow remarried (This probably refers to a girl married in her infancy, or when very young and whose husband had died before she arrived at the age of puberty. Infant marriages are still prevelant among some sections of Hindus.) or a concubine, should lead a chaste life, devoted to her husband, and doing everything for his welfare. Women acting thus acquire Dharma, Artha, and Kama, obtain a high position, and generally keep their husbands devoted to them.

THE CONDUCT OF THE ELDER WIFE

From the very beginning, a wife should attract her husband, by showing her devotion, her good temper, and her practical common sense. Unfortunately if she cannot conceive, she should herself tell her husband to marry another woman. And when the second wife is married, and brought to the house, the first wife should give her a position superior to her own, and look upon her as a sister.

marriage

In the morning the elder wife should forcibly make the younger one decorate herself in the presence of their husband, and should not mind all the husband's favour being given to her. If the younger wife does anything to displease her husband the elder one should not neglect her, but should always be ready to give her most careful advice, and should teach her to do various things in the presence of her husband. She should treat the children as her own, her attendants she should look upon with more regard, even than on her own servants, her friends she should cherish with love and kindness, and her relations with great honour.

When there are many other wives beside herself, the eldest wife should be close with the one who is immediately next to her in rank and age, and should instigate the wife who had recently enjoyed her husband's favour to quarrel with the youngest favourite. After this she should sympathize with the former, and having collected all the other wives together, should get them to denounce the favourite as a scheming and wicked woman, without however committing herself in any way. If the favourite wife happens to quarrel with the husband, then the elder wife should take her part and give her false encouragement, and thus cause the quarrel to be increased. But if after all this she finds the husband still continues to love his favourite wife she should then change her tactics, and endeavour to bring about a conciliation between them, so as to avoid her husband's displeasure.

THE CONDUCT OF THE YOUNGER WIFE

The younger wife should regard the elder wife of her husband as her mother, and should not give anything away, even to her own relations, without her knowledge. She should tell her everything about herself, and not approach her husband without her permission. Whatever is told to her by the elder wife she should not reveal to others, and she should take care of the children of the senior even more than of her own. When alone with her husband she should serve him well, but should not tell him of the pain she suffers from the existence of a rival wife. She may also obtain secretly from her husband some marks of his particular regard for her, and may tell him that she lives only for him, and for the regard that he has for her. She should never reveal her love for her husband, nor her husband's

(Facing page)
A virtuous woman, who has affection of her husband, should act according to his wishes as if he were a divine being. She should keep the house neat and clean; arrange flowers of various kinds in different parts of the house. She should keep herself well groomed, with different hairstyles, jewellery and fresh set of clothes and wait for him at the door in order to greet him when he returns

(Following pages)
Man married to many wives should act fairly towards all of them. He should show his passion towards all his wives and not restrict it to just one. He should amuse them all by taking them to the garden, by lavishing presents on them and enjoying them in loving unions

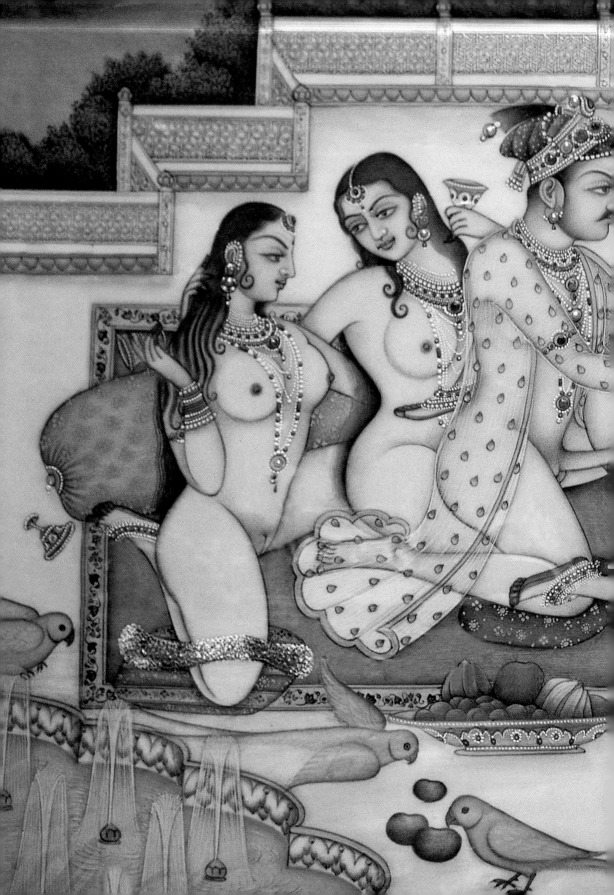

When the woman places one of her legs on her lover's shoulder, and stretches out the other, and then places on his other shoulder and does it alternately, it is called the 'splitting of a bamboo'. When one of her legs is placed on the head, and the other is stretched out, it is called the 'fixing of a nail'

love for her to any person, either in pride or in anger, for a wife that reveals the secrets of her husband is despised by him. As for seeking to obtain the regard of her husband, Gonardiya says, that it should always be done in private, for fear of the elder wife. If the elder wife be disliked by her husband, or be childless, she should sympathize with her, and should ask her husband to do the same, but should surpass her in leading the life of a chaste woman.

THE CONDUCT OF A VIRGIN WIDOW REMARRIED

A widow in poor circumstances, who allies herself again to a man, is called a widow remarried. A virgin widow should not marry a person whom she may be obliged to leave on account of his bad character, or of his being destitute. The cause of a widow's marrying again is her desire for happiness, and as happiness is secured because of qualities in her husband, joined to love of enjoyment, it is better therefore to secure a person endowed with such qualities in the first instance. Vatsyayana thinks that a widow may marry any person that she likes, and that she thinks will suit her.

At the time of her marriage the widow should obtain from her husband the money to pay the cost of drinking parties, and picnics with her relations, and of giving them and her friends kindly gifts and presents; or she may do these things at her own cost if she likes. In the same way she may wear either her husband's ornaments or her own. As to the presents of affection mutually exchanged between the husband and herself there is no fixed rule about them. If she leaves her husband after marriage of her own accord, she should restore to him whatever he may have given her, with the exception of the mutual presents. If however she is driven out of the house by her husband she should not return anything to him.

After her marriage she should live in the house of her husband like one of the chief members of the family, but should treat the other ladies of the family with kindness, the servants with generosity, and all the friends of the house with familiarity and good temper. She should show that she is better acquainted with the sixty-four arts than the other ladies of the house, and in any quarrels with her husband she should not rebuke him severely but in private do everything that he wishes, and make use of the sixty-four ways of enjoyment. She should be obliging to the other wives of her

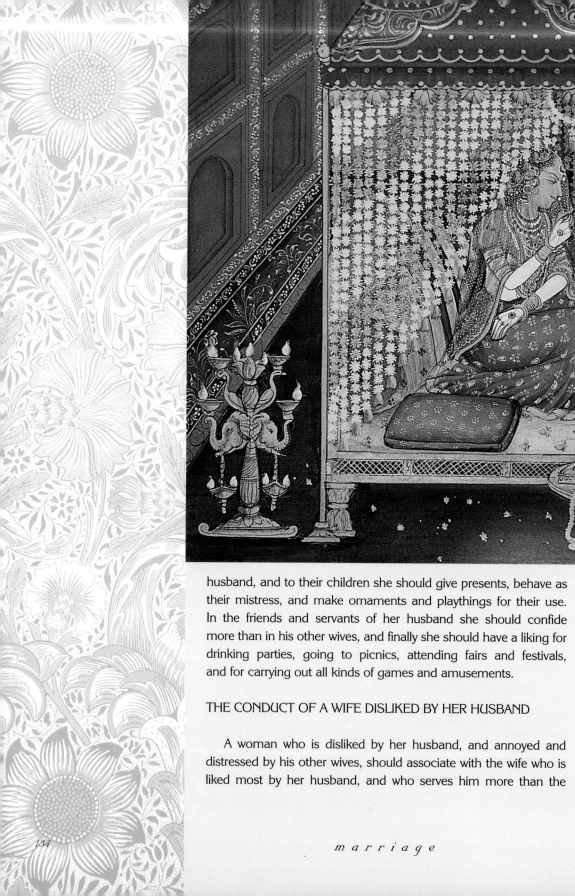

husband, and to their children she should give presents, behave as
their mistress, and make ornaments and playthings for their use.
In the friends and servants of her husband she should confide
more than in his other wives, and finally she should have a liking for
drinking parties, going to picnics, attending fairs and festivals,
and for carrying out all kinds of games and amusements.

THE CONDUCT OF A WIFE DISLIKED BY HER HUSBAND

A woman who is disliked by her husband, and annoyed and
distressed by his other wives, should associate with the wife who is
liked most by her husband, and who serves him more than the

marriage

This miniature shows a newly wedded bride waiting for her husband on their first night. On such occasions the bed is surrounded by jasmine flowers and is covered with the rose petals, the bride is shyly covering her face with her scarf; her husband will beg her to take it off for the night

others, and should teach her all the arts with which she is acquaint-ed. She should act as the nurse to her husband's children, and having gained over his friends to her side, should through them make him acquainted of her devotion to him. In religious cere-monies she should be a leader, as also in vows and fasts, and should not hold too good an opinion of herself. When her husband is lying on his bed she should only go near him when it is agreeable to him, and should never rebuke him, or be obstinate in any way. If her husband happens to quarrel with any of his other wives, she should reconcile them to each other, and if he desires to see any woman secretly, she should manage to bring about the meeting between them. She should moreover make herself acquainted with the

marriage

weak points of her husband's character, but always keep them secret, and on the whole behave herself in such a way as may lead him to look upon her as a good and devoted wife.

ON THE CONDUCT OF THE KING WITH THE WIVES AND CONCUBINES

The female attendants in the harem should bring flowers, ointments and clothes from the king's wives to the king, and he having received these things should give them as presents to the servants, along with the things worn by him the previous day. In the afternoon the king, having dressed and put on his ornaments, should interview the women of the harem, who should also be dressed and decorated with jewels. Then having given to each of them respect as may suit the occasion and as they may deserve, he should carry on with them a cheerful conversation. Later he should visit his wives as may be virgin widows remarried, concubines and dancing girls in their private rooms.

When the king rises from his noonday sleep, the woman whose duty it is to inform the king regarding the wife who is to spend the night with him should come to him along with the female attendants. These attendants should place before the king the ointments and unguents sent by each of these wives, marked with the seal of her ring, and their names and their reasons for sending the ointments should be told to the king. After this the king accepts the ointment of one of them, who then is informed that her ointment has been accepted, and that her day has been settled.

At festivals, singing parties and exhibitions, all the wives of the king should be treated with respect and served with drinks. But the women of the harem should not be allowed to go out alone, neither should any women outside the harem be allowed to enter it except those whose character is well known. And lastly the work which the king's wives have to do should not be too fatiguing.

THE CONDUCT OF A HUSBAND TOWARDS MANY WIVES

A man marrying many wives should act fairly towards them all. He should neither disregard nor pass over their faults, and should

not reveal to one wife the love, passion, bodily blemishes and
confidential reproaches of the other. No opportunity should be
given to any one of them of speaking to him about their rivals, and
if one of them should begin to speak ill of another, he should chide
her and tell her that she has exactly the same blemishes in her
character. One of them he should please by secret confidence,
another by secret respect, and another by secret flattery, and
he should please them all by going to gardens, by presents,
by honouring their relations, by telling them secrets, and lastly
by loving unions. A young woman who is of a good temper, and
who conducts herself according to the precepts of the Holy Writ,
wins her husband's love and affection.

marriage

OTHER WIVES

The wives of other people may be resorted to on the occasions already described in first chapter, but the possibility of their acquisition, their fitness for cohabitation, the danger to oneself in uniting with them, should first of all be examined. A man may resort to the wife of another, for the purpose of saving his own life, when he perceives that his love for her proceeds from one degree of intensity to another. These degrees are ten in number, and are distinguished by the following signs:

Ancient authors believe that a man should know the disposition, truthfulness, purity, and will of a young woman, as also the intensity, or weakness of her passions, from the form of her body, and from her characteristic marks and signs. But Vatsyayana is of opinion that the forms of bodies, and the characteristic marks or signs are but erring tests of character, and that women should be judged by their conduct, by the outward expression of their thoughts, and by the movements of their bodies.

Now as a general rule Gonikaputra says that a woman falls in love with every handsome man she sees, and so does every man at the sight of a beautiful woman, but frequently they do not take any further steps, owing to various considerations. In love the following circumstances are peculiar to the woman. She loves without regard to right or wrong, and does not try to gain over a man simply for the attainment of some particular purpose. Moreover, when a man first makes up to her she naturally shrinks from him, even though she may be willing to unite herself with him. But when the attempts to gain her are repeated and renewed, she consents at last.

But with a man, even though he may have begun to love, he conquers his feelings from a regard for morality and wisdom, and although his thoughts are often on the woman, he does not yield, even though an attempt be made to gain him over. He sometimes makes an attempt or effort to win the object of his affections, and having failed, he leaves her alone for the future. In the same way, when a woman is won over, he often becomes indifferent about her. The belief that a man does not care for what is easily gained, and only desires a thing which cannot be obtained without difficulty, is not true.

marriage

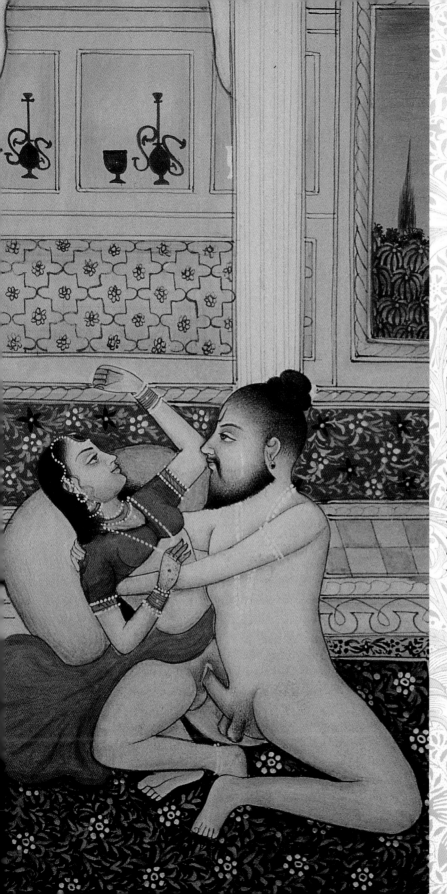

Sexual intercourse can be compared to a quarrel, on account of contrarieties of love and its tendency to dispute. The place of striking with passion is the body. Blows with the hand should be given on the back of the woman while she is sitting on the lap of a man, and she should give blows in return, abusing the man as if she were angry

As a rule a woman falls in love with every handsome man she sees, and so does every man at the sight of a beautiful woman, but owing to various circumstances they hardly take any further step. A woman loves without the regard of right or wrong, she does not try to win over a man just for fulfilling her carnal desires

The causes of a woman rejecting the addresses of a man could be any one of the following: Affection for her husband; desire of lawful progeny; want of opportunity; anger at being addressed by the man too familiarly; difference in status; thinking that the man may be attached to some other person; fear of the man's not keeping his intentions secret; thinking that the man is too devoted to his friends, and has too great a regard for them; bashfulness on account of his being an illustrious man; fear on account of his being powerful, or possessed of too impetuous passion, in the case of the deer woman; in the case of an elephant woman, the thought that he is a hare man, or a man of weak passion; disillusion at seeing his grey hair or shabby appearance; fear that he may be employed by her husband to test her chastity and so on.

Whichever of the above causes a man may detect, he should endeavour to remove it from the very beginning. Thus, the bashfulness that may arise from his greatness or his ability, he should remove by showing his great love and affection for her. The difficulty of the want of opportunity, or of his inaccessibility, he should remove by showing her some easy way of access. The excessive respect entertained by the woman for him should be removed by making himself very familiar. The difficulties that arise from his being thought a low character he should remove by showing his valour and his wisdom; those that come from neglect by extra attention; and those that arise from fear by giving her proper encouragement.

The men who generally succeed with women are those who are well versed in the science of love, who have the way with words (gift of the gab). Those who are acquainted with women from their childhood; and those who have secured their confidence professionally and economically.

Men who are devoted to sexual pleasures, even though these be with their own servants.

Men who have been lately married. Men who like picnics and pleasure parties. Men who are celebrated for being very strong (Bull men). Men who surpass their husbands in learning and good looks, in good qualities, and in liberality.

The women who are easily gained over are those, who stand at the doors of their houses and always looking out on the street. A woman that stares at you or looks sideways at you. A woman whose husband has taken another wife without any reason.

A woman who hates her husband, or who is hated by him. A woman who has nobody to look after her, or keep her in check. A woman who has not had any children. A woman who is social climber. A woman who is apparently very affectionate with her husband. And finally, wife of an actor. These kinds of women are more receptive to the advances of a man who has studied sixty-four arts.

'Desire, which springs from nature, and which is increased by art, and from which all danger is taken away by wisdom, becomes firm and secure. A clever man, depending on his own ability, and observing carefully the ideas and thoughts of women, and removing the causes of their turning away from men, is generally successful with them.

THE WAYS OF MAKING THE ACQUAINTANCE OF WOMAN DESIRED

This author is of the opinion that girls are not so easily seduced by employing female messengers as by the efforts of the man himself, but that the wives of others are more easily got at by the aid of female messengers than by the personal efforts of the man. Vatsyayana says that whenever it is possible a man should always act by himself in these matters, and it is only when such is impossible, that female messengers should be employed. The belief that women who act and talk boldly and freely are to be won by the personal efforts of the man, and that women who do not possess those qualities can be got at by female messengers, does not hold any ground.

A man should first of all make the acquaintance of the woman he loves in the following manner:

He should see the woman either on a natural or special opportunity. A natural opportunity is when one of them goes to the house of the other, and a special opportunity is when they meet either at the house of a friend, or caste member, or a minister, or a physician, and also on the occasion of marriage ceremonies, sacrifices, festivals, funerals, and garden parties.

When they do meet, the man should look at her in such a way as to make his intentions known to her; he should pull about his moustache, make a sound with his nails, and cause his own ornaments to tinkle, bite his lower lip, and make various other signs of that description. When she is looking at him he should speak

marriage

Ancient authors believe that a man should know the disposition, truthfulness, intensity and weakness of the passion of a young woman from the form of her body and her characteristic signs

to his friends about her and other women, and should show to her his liberality and his appreciation of enjoyments. When sitting by the side of a female friend he should yawn and twist his body, contract his eyebrows, speak very slowly as if he was weary, and listen to her indifferently.

A subtle conversation having two meanings should also be carried on with a child or some other person, apparently having regard to a third person, but really having reference to the woman he loves. He should make his love manifest by referring to others rater than to herself. He should embrace and kiss a child in her presence, and give it the mixture of betel nuts with his tongue, and press its chin with his fingers in a caressing way. All these things should be done at the proper time and in proper places.

marriage

The man should fondle a child that may be sitting on her lap, and give it something to play with. Conversation with respect to the child may also be held with her, and in this manner he should gradually become well acquainted with her, and he should also make himself agreeable to her relations. Afterwards, this acquaintance should be made a pretext for visiting her house frequently, and on such occasions he should converse on the subject of love in her absence but within her hearing.

As his intimacy with her increases he should place in her charge some kind of deposit or trust, and take away from it a small portion at a time; or he may give her some fragrant substances, or betel nuts to be kept for him by her.

After this he should endeavour to make her well acquainted with his own wife, and get them to carry on confidential conversations, and to sit together in lonely places. In order to see her frequently he should arrange so that the two families should employ the same goldsmith, the same jeweller, the same basket maker, the same dyer, and the same washer man. And he should also pay her long visits openly under the pretence of being engaged with her on business, and one business should lead to another, so as to keep up the intercourse between them.

Whenever she wants anything, or is in need of money, or wishes to acquire skill in one of the arts, he should make her feel that he is willing and able to do anything that she wants, to give her money, or teach her one of the arts, all these things being quite within his ability and power. In the same way he should hold discussions with her in company with other people, and they should talk of the doings and sayings of other persons, and examine different things, like jewellery, precious stones, etc. On such occasions he should show her certain things with the values of which she may be unacquainted, and if she begins to dispute with him about the things or their value, he should not contradict her, but point out that he agrees with her in every way.

After a girl has become acquainted with the man as above described, and has manifested her love to him by the various outward signs and by the motions of her body, the man should make every effort to gain her over. But as girls are not acquainted with sexual union, they should be treated with the greatest delicacy, and the man should proceed with considerable caution, though in the case of other women, accustomed to sexual intercourse, this is not necessary. When the intentions of the girl are known, and her bashfulness put aside, the man should begin to make use of her money, and an interchange of clothes and flowers should be made.

When a man is endeavouring to seduce one woman, he should not attempt to seduce any other at the same time. But after he has succeeded with the first, and enjoyed her for a considerable time, he can keep her affections by giving her presents that she likes, and then commence making up to another woman. A wise man having a regard for his reputation should not think of seducing a woman who is apprehensive, timid, not to be trusted, well guarded, or has of a father-in-law or mother-in-law.

EXAMINATION OF THE STATE OF A WOMAN'S MIND

When a man is trying to win over a woman he should examine the state of her mind, and act as follows: If she listens to him,

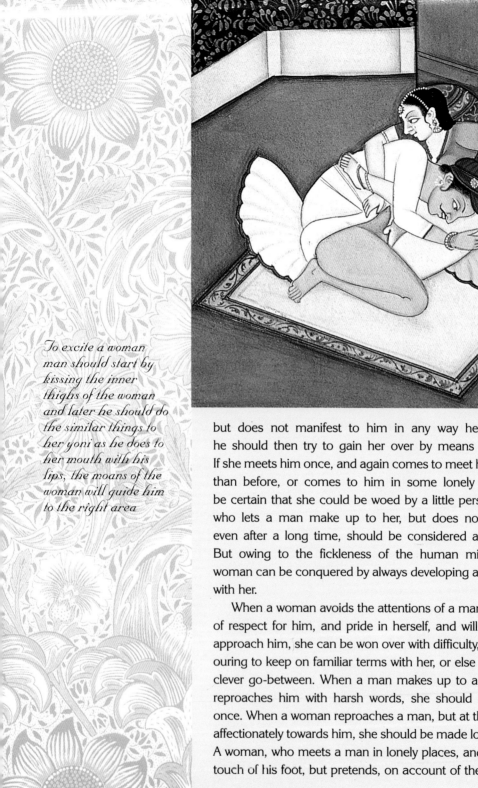

To excite a woman man should start by kissing the inner thighs of the woman and later he should do the similar things to her yoni as he does to her mouth with his lips, the moans of the woman will guide him to the right area

but does not manifest to him in any way her own intentions, he should then try to gain her over by means of a go-between. If she meets him once, and again comes to meet him better dressed than before, or comes to him in some lonely place, he should be certain that she could be woed by a little persuasion. A woman who lets a man make up to her, but does not give herself up, even after a long time, should be considered as a fickle in love. But owing to the fickleness of the human mind, even such a woman can be conquered by always developing a close relationship with her.

When a woman avoids the attentions of a man, and on account of respect for him, and pride in herself, and will not meet him or approach him, she can be won over with difficulty, either by endeavouring to keep on familiar terms with her, or else by an exceedingly clever go-between. When a man makes up to a woman, and she reproaches him with harsh words, she should be abandoned at once. When a woman reproaches a man, but at the same time acts affectionately towards him, she should be made love to in every way. A woman, who meets a man in lonely places, and puts up with the touch of his foot, but pretends, on account of the indecision of her

marriage

mind, not to be aware of it, should be conquered by patience, and by continued efforts as follows:

If she happens to go to sleep in his vicinity he should put his left arm round her, and see when she awakes whether she repulses him in reality, or only repulses him in such a way as if she was desirous of the same thing being done to her again. And what is done by the arm can also be done by the foot. If the man succeeds in this point he should embrace her more closely, and if she will not stand the embrace and gets up, but behaves with him as usual the next day, he should consider then that she is not unwilling to be enjoyed by him. If however she does not appear again, the man should try to get over her by means of a go-between; and if, after having disappeared for some time, she again appears, and behaves with him as usual, the man should then consider that she would not object to be united with him. When a woman gives a man an opportunity, and makes her own love manifest to him, he should proceed to enjoy her. And the signs of a woman manifesting her love are these: She calls out to a man without being addressed by him in the first instance.

She shows herself to him in secret places. She speaks to him

tremblingly and inarticulately. She has the fingers of her hand, and the toes of her feet moistened with perspiration, and her face blooming with delight. She occupies herself with rubbing his body and pressing his head. When rubbing him down she works with one hand only, and with the other she touches and embraces parts of his body. She remains still with both hands placed on his body as if she had been surprised by something, or was overcome by fatigue. She sometimes bends down her face upon his thighs and, when asked to rub them does not manifest any unwillingness to do so. She places one of her hands quite motionless on his body, and even though the man should press it between two members of his body, she does not remove it for a long time. Lastly, when she has resisted all the efforts of the man to gain her over, she returns to him next day to massage his body as before.

When a woman neither gives encouragement to a man, nor avoids him, but hides herself and remains in some lonely place, she must be got at by means of the female servant who may be near her. If when called by the man she acts in the same way, then she should be won by means of a skilful go-between. But if she will have nothing to say to the man, he should consider well about her before he begins any further attempts to gain her over.

THE BEHAVIOUR OF THE WOMAN WITH THE GO-BETWEEN

If a woman has manifested her love or desire, either by signs or by motions of the body, then the man should get a go-between to approach her.

The go-between should get herself into the confidence of the woman by visiting her house and taking expensive gifts to her on behalf of her master. When the woman manifests her love in the manner above described, the go-between should increase it by bringing to her love tokens from the man. The go-between should further talk to the woman about the weakness of the passion of her husband, all the other faults that he may have, and with which she may be acquainted. If the wife be a deer woman, and the husband a hare man, then there would be no fault in that direction, but in the event of his being a hare man, and she a mare woman or elephant woman, then this fault should be pointed out to her.

For the first three days after the marriage, the girl and her husband should sleep on the floor and abstain from sexual pleasures. For the next seven days they should bathe to the sound of musical instruments, decorate themselves, eat together. On the tenth day, after gaining confidence of the bride, he should take her to some lonely place and enjoy her

'A man should first get himself introduced to a woman,

and then carry on a conversation with her.

He should give her hints of his love for her,

and if he finds from her replies that she receives these hints favourably,

he should then set to work to gain her over without any fear.

A woman who shows her love by outward signs to the man at his first interview

should be gained over very easily.

In the same way a lascivious woman,

who when addressed in loving words replies openly

in words expressive of her love, should be considered

to have been gained over at that very moment.

With regard to all women, whether they be wise, simple, or confiding,

this rule is laid down that those who make an open manifestation

of their love are easily gained over.'

other men's wives

*T*he common people constantly emulate Kings and their ministers' lives. Hence it is imperative for the persons in authority to set a moral example for the ordinary citizens.

The village head, the king's officer and the storekeeper can win over female villagers simply by asking them. These classes of woman are called unchaste women by over sexed men given to sexual pleasures.

These men take advantage of these women who are poor and do menial jobs. In the same way the superintendents of cow pens enjoy the women in the cow pens; and the officers, who look after widows, women who are without supporters, and women who have left their husbands, have sexual intercourse with them. The intelligent accomplish their object by wandering at night in the village, and while villagers also unite with the wives of their sons, being much alone with them. Lastly the superintendents of markets have a great deal to do with the female villagers at the time of their making purchases in the market.

During festivals, women of cities and towns generally visit the women in the royal palace. On such occasions a female attendant of the king (previously acquainted with the woman whom the king desires) should wait about, and approach the woman and persuade her to come and see the royal palace. She should show her the garden with its floor inlaid with precious stones, and the fruit orchards. She should also show her the royal vaults where all kinds of treasures are hidden. When alone with her, she should tell her about the love of the king for her, and the good fortune which would attend upon her, on her union with the king, giving her at the time a strict promise of secrecy. If the woman does not accept the offer, she should conciliate and please her with handsome presents befitting the position of the king, and having accompanied her for some distance should dismiss her with great affection.

Or, a female beggar, in league with the king's wife, should say to the woman desired by the king, and whose husband may have lost his wealth, or may have some cause of fear from the king: 'This wife of the king has influence over him, and she is, moreover, naturally kind-hearted, we must therefore go to her in this matter. I shall arrange for your entrance into the harem, and

Men in authority sexually exploit women who are poor and do menial jobs; women without families; women separated from their husbands and women who are virgin widows

other men's wives

she will do away with all cause of danger and fear from the king.'

The same modus operendi can be also be used by the wives of those who seek favours from the king.

The above mentioned ways of gaining over the wives of other men are chiefly practised in the palaces of kings. But a king should never enter the abode of another person, for Abhira the king of the Kottas, was killed by a washer man while in the house of another, and in the same way Jayasana, the king of the Kashis, was slain by the commandant of his cavalry.

According to the customs of some countries there are facilities for kings to make love to the wives of other men. Thus in the country of the Andhras the newly married daughters of the people thereof enter the king's harem with some presents on the tenth day of their marriage, and having been enjoyed by the king are then dismissed. In the country of the Vatsagulmas the wives of the chief ministers approach the king at night to serve him. In the country of the Vaidarbhas the beautiful wives of the inhabitants pass a month in the king's harem under the pretence of affection for the king. In the country of the Aparatakas the people gave their beautiful wives as presents to the ministers and the kings. And lastly in the country of the Saurashtras the women of the city and the country enter the royal harem for the king's pleasure either together or separately.

'The above and other ways are the means employed in different countries by kings with regard to the wives of other persons. But a king, who has the welfare of his people at heart, should not on any account put them into practice.'

'A king, who has conquered the six enemies (Lust, Anger, Avarice, Spiritual Ignorance, Pride, and Envy) of mankind, becomes the master of the whole earth.'

THE WOMEN OF THE ROYAL HAREM

The women of the royal harem cannot meet any men as they are strictly guarded, neither do they have their desires satisfied, because their only husband is common to many wives. For this reason they give pleasure to each other in various ways.

Having dressed their female friends, or their female attendants, like men, they accomplish their object by means of bulbs,

A Rajasthani miniature portrays a man enjoying his two wives in his palace which is beautifully decorated to create a sensual ambience.

other men's wives

roots, and fruits having the form of the lingam, or they lie down upon the statue of a male figure, in which the lingam is visible and erect.

Some kings, who are compassionate, take or apply certain medicines to enable them to enjoy many wives in one night, for the purpose of satisfying the desire of their women, though they perhaps have no desire of their own. Others enjoy with great affection only those wives that they particularly like, while others have to wait for their turn.

The ladies of the royal harem, with the help of their female attendants, secretly admit men in the disguise of women in their apartments. Their female attendants and the daughters of their nurses, who are acquainted with their secrets, have to exert themselves to get men to come to the harem. The men should be lured in with the promise of rich rewards and making them aware of poorly guarded passages to come in and escape from. But these women should never induce a man to enter the harem by telling him lies, for if he is caught, he will be killed.

As for the man himself he had better not enter a royal harem, even though it may be easily accessible, on account of the numerous disasters to which he may be exposed there. If however he wants to enter it, he should first ascertain whether there is an easy way to get out, whether it is closely surrounded by the pleasure garden, whether it has separate enclosures belonging to it, whether the sentinels are careless, whether the king has gone abroad, and then, when he is called by the women of the harem, he should carefully observe the localities, and enter by the way pointed out by them. If he is able to manage it, he should hang about the harem every day, and under some pretext or other, make friends with the sentinels, and show himself attached to the female attendants of the harem, who may have become acquainted with his design, and to whom he should express his regret at not being able to obtain the object of his desire. Lastly the go-between should be a woman who has access to the harem, and he should be careful to be able to recognize the emissaries of the king.

He should disguise himself as a female attendant of the lady who comes to the place, or passes by it. When she looks at him he should let her know his feelings by outward signs and gestures,

other men's wives

A temple carving from South India showing a man enjoying his woman like a bull mounts a cow. Seated below is the maid servant who is giving support to the woman

159

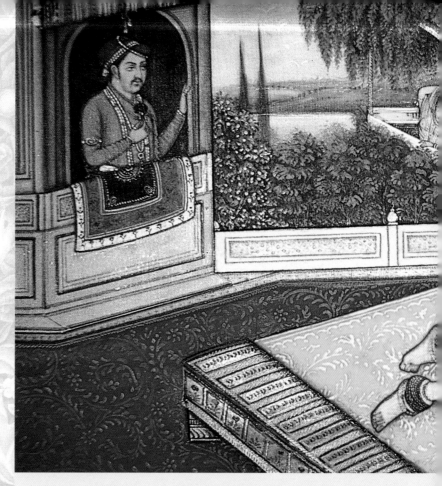

and should show her pictures, things with double meanings,
chaplets of flowers, and rings. He should carefully mark the
answer she gives, whether by word or by sign, or by gesture, and
should then try and get into the harem. If he is certain of her coming to some particular place he should conceal himself there, and
at the appointed time should enter along with her as one of the
guards. He may also go in and out, concealed in a folded bed, or
bed covering, or with his body made invisible, by means of external applications, a receipt for one of which is as follows:

The heart of an ichneumon fly, the fruit of the long gourd
(tumbi), and the eyes of a serpent should all be burnt without
letting out the smoke. The ashes should then be ground and
mixed in equal quantities with water. By putting this mixture upon
the eyes a man can go about unseen.

The entrance of young men into harems, and their exit from
them, generally take place when things are being brought in or
taken out of palace, or when drinking festivals are going on, or

A woman whose husband has violated the chastity of many wives should be paid back in the same coin. A woman who has been enjoyed by five men is a fit and proper person to be enjoyed. A man can be seen lustfully eying his neighbour's wife from his window

when the female attendants are in a hurry, or when the residence of some of the royal ladies is being changed, or when the king's wives go to gardens, or when they enter the palace on their return from them, or lastly, when the king is absent on a long pilgrimage. The women of the royal harem know each other's secrets, and having but one object to attain, they give assistance to each other. A young man, who enjoys all of them, and who is common to them all, can continue enjoying his union with them so long as it is kept quiet.

In the country of the Aparatakas the royal ladies are not well protected, and consequently many young men are passed into the harem by the women of the royal palace. The wives of the king of the Ahira country accomplish their objects with those sentinels in the harem who bear the name of Kshatriyas. The royal ladies in the country of the Vatsagulmas cause such men as are suitable to enter into the harem along with their female messengers. In the country of the Vaidarbhas the sons of the

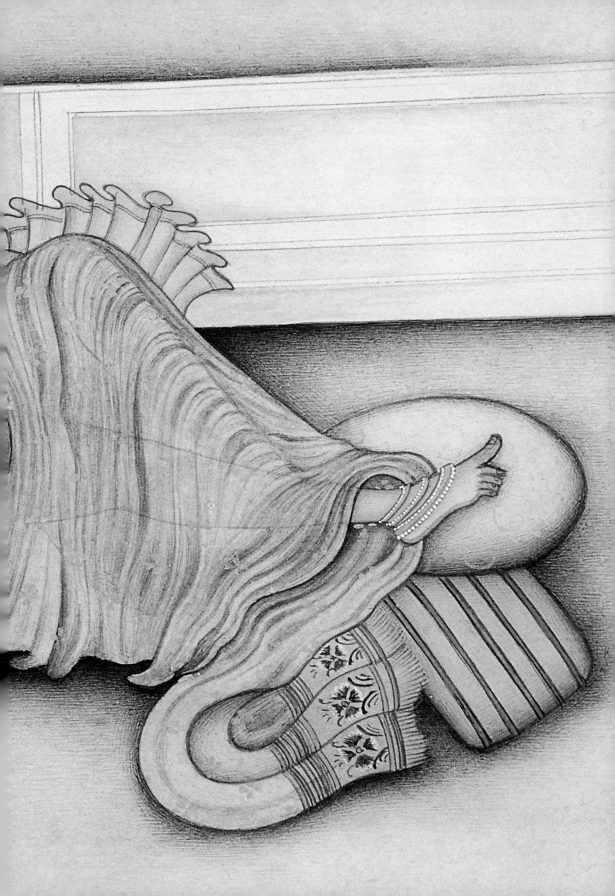

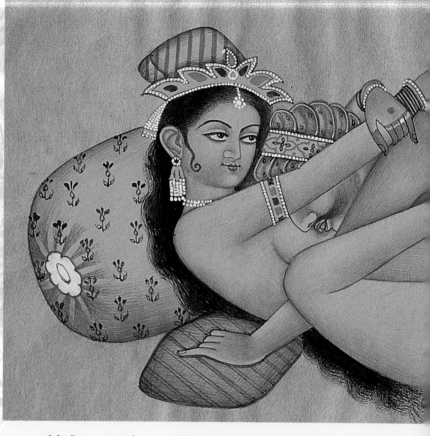

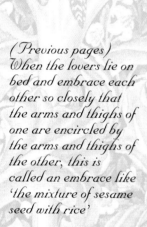

(Previous pages) When the lovers lie on bed and embrace each other so closely that the arms and thighs of one are encircled by the arms and thighs of the other, this is called an embrace like 'the mixture of sesame seed with rice'

royal ladies enter the royal harem when they please and enjoy the women. In the Stri-rajya the wives of the king are enjoyed by his caste fellows and relations. In the Ganda country the royal wives are enjoyed by Brahmins, friends, servants and slaves. In the Samdhava country servants, foster children and other persons like them enjoy the women of the harem. In the country of the Haimavatas adventurous citizens bribe the sentinels and enter the harem. In the country of the Vanyas and the Kalmyas, Brahmins, with the knowledge of the king, enter the harem under the pretence of giving flowers to the ladies, and speak with them from behind a curtain, and from such conversation union afterwards takes place. Lastly, the women in the harem of the king of the Prachyas conceal one young man in the harem for every batch of nine or ten of the women.

LOOKING AFTER ONE'S OWN WIFE

For these reasons a man should guard his own wife. Old authors say that a king should select for sentinels in his harem

other men's wives

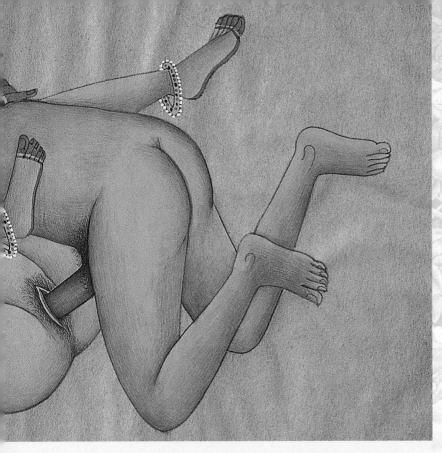

When love becomes
intense, scratching
with nails or biting is
practised and is done
on the first visit;
at the time of setting
out on a journey;
when angry lover is
reconciled and lastly
when the woman is
intoxicated

such men as have their freedom from carnal desires well tested. But such men, though free themselves from carnal desire, by reason of their fear or greed, may cause other persons to enter the harem, and therefore Gonikaputra says that kings should place such men in the harem as may have had their freedom from carnal desires, their fears, and their avarice well tested. Lastly, the followers of Babhravya say that a man should cause his wife to associate with a young woman who would tell him the secrets of other people and thus find out from her about his wife's chastity. But Vatsyayana says that as wicked persons are always successful with women, a man should not cause his innocent wife to be corrupted by bringing her into the company of a deceitful woman.

The following are the causes of the destruction of a woman's chastity: always going into society and sitting in company; absence of restraint; the loose habits of her husband; want of caution in her relations with other men; continued and long absence of her husband; living in a foreign country; destruction of her love and feelings by her husband; the company of loose women and the jealousy of her husband.

'A clever man, learning from the Shastras

the ways of winning over the wives of other people,

is never deceived in the case of his own wives.

No one, however, should make use of these ways for seducing

the wives of others, because they do not always succeed, and,

moreover, often cause disasters, and the destruction of Dharma and Artha.

This book, which is intended for the good of the people, and to teach them the

ways of guarding their own wives,

should not be made use of merely for gaining over the wives of others.'

courtesan

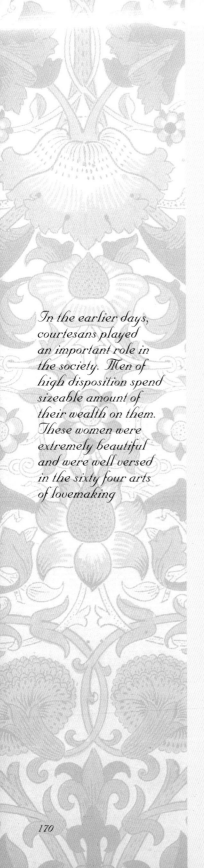

*In the earlier days,
courtesans played
an important role in
the society. Men of
high disposition spend
sizeable amount of
their wealth on them.
These women were
extremely beautiful
and were well versed
in the sixty four arts
of lovemaking*

T he study of the social life of the early Hindus would not be complete without mention of the courtesan. Hindus have always accepted the courtesan as an integral part of human society, and so long as they behaved themselves with decency and propriety they were treated with certain respect. Anyhow, they have never been treated in the East with that brutality and contempt so common in the West, while their education has always been of a superior kind to that bestowed upon the rest of womankind in Oriental countries.

In the earlier days the well educated Hindu dancing girl and courtesan doubtless resembled the Hetera of the Greeks, and, being educated and amusing, far more acceptable as companions than the married or unmarried women were. At all times and in all countries, there has always been a rivalry between the chaste and the unchaste. But while some women are born courtesans, and follow the instincts of their nature in every class of society, it has been truly said by some authors that every woman has got an inkling of the profession in her nature, and does her best to make herself agreeable to the male sex.

A courtesan should be beautiful, and amiable, with auspicious body marks. She should have a liking for good qualities in other people, as also a liking for wealth. She should take delight in sexual unions, resulting from love, and should be of a firm mind, and of the same class as the man with regard to sexual enjoyment. She should always be anxious to acquire and obtain experience and knowledge, be free from avarice, and always have a liking for social gatherings, and for the arts.

The following are the ordinary qualities of all women: intelligence, good disposition and good manners; to be straightforward in behaviour, and to be grateful; to consider well the future before doing anything; to possess activity, to be of consistent behaviour, and to have a knowledge of the proper times and places for doing things; to speak always without meanness, loud laughter, malignity, anger, avarice, dullness, or stupidity; to have a knowledge of the Kamasutra, and to be skilled in all the arts connected with it.

The subtlety of women, their wonderful perceptive powers, their knowledge, and their intuitive appreciation of men and things are all mentioned here, which may be looked upon as a quintessence worked up into detail by many writers in every quarter of the world.

FAVOURITE LOVER

By having intercourse with men, courtesans not only get sexual pleasure but also a maintenance. When she treats the man with love, the action is natural; but when the purpose is of getting money, her action is artificial. Even in the latter case, however, she should pretend as if her love were indeed natural, because men repose their confidence on those women who apparently love them. In making known her love to the man, she should not show herself as greedy, and for the sake of her future she should abstain from acquiring money from him by unlawful means.

A courtesan, beautifully dressed and laden with jewels, should sit or stand at the door of her house, without exposing herself too much. She should look on the public road so as to be seen by the

c o u r t e s a n

This fabulous sculpture adorns the walls of the magnificent Kandharia Mahadev Temple at Khajuraho. It shows a tantrik yogi, in shirsha asana or head stand position copulating with a woman. This difficult position was achieved with the help of the attendants who can be seen on the either side, yogi is satisfying them by using his fingers

passersby, for she is an object on sale. She should form friendships with such persons as would enable her to attract men from other women and attach them to herself, to repair her own misfortunes, to acquire wealth. To protect herself from being bullied, she should charm police officers and judges. For acquiring wealth she should shower her affection on men who hold good positions or those who have unfailing sources of income. Also a son of a wealthy person, men who consider themselves important and king's physician are a good catch.

On the other hand, those who are possessed of excellent qualities are to be resorted to for the sake of love and fame. Such men are those of high birth, learned, with a good knowledge of the world, and doing the proper things at the proper times, poets, good story tellers, eloquent men, energetic men, skilled in various arts,

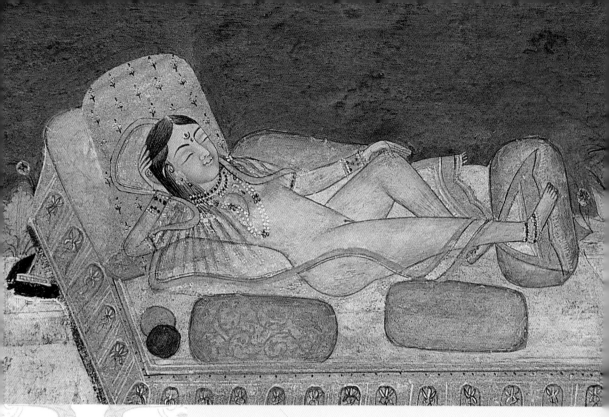

The courtesan or
Veshya was an
important element of
Hindu society till the
colonial period; her
intellect and beauty
were far superior to
the women of the
household

far-seeing into the future, possessed of great minds, full of perse-
verance, of a firm devotion, free from anger, liberal, affectionate to
their parents, and with a liking for all social gatherings, skilled in
completing verses begun by others and in various other sports, free
from all disease, possessed of a perfect body, strong, and not addicted to drinking, powerful in sexual enjoyment, sociable, showing love
towards women and attracting their hearts to himself, but not entire-
ly devoted to them, possessed of independent means of livelihood,
free from envy, and last of all, free from suspicion.

Courtesans should avoid men who are unhealthy in both body
and mind. Men who are greedy, pitiless, conceited, and those
who have no self-respect and courtesy towards others should also
be avoided.

A courtesan should not sacrifice money to her love, because
money is the chief thing to be attended to. But in cases of fear, etc.,
she should pay regard to strength and other qualities. Moreover,
even though she be invited by any man to join him, she should not
at once consent to a union, because men are apt to despise things
which are easily acquired. On such occasions she should first send
the others who may be in her service, or, in their absence the
Pithamardas, or confidants, to find out the state of his feelings,

c o u r t e s a n

and the condition of his mind. By means of these persons she should ascertain whether the man is pure or impure, affected, or the reverse, capable of attachment, or indifferent, liberal or niggardly; and if she finds him to her liking, she should then employ the Vita and others to attach his mind to her.

Accordingly, the Pithamarda should bring the man to her house, under the pretence of seeing the fights of quails, cocks, and rams, of hearing the mania (a kind of starling) talk, or of seeing some other spectacle, or the practice of some art; or he may take the woman to the abode of the man. After this, when the man comes to her house the woman should give him something to provoke his curiosity and love, such as an affectionate present, telling him that it was specially designed for his use. She should also amuse him for a long time by telling him such stories, and doing such things as he may take most delight in. When he goes away she should frequently send him a female attendant, skilled in carrying on an amusing conversation, and also a small present at the same time. She should also sometimes go to him herself under the pretence of some business, and accompanied by the Pithamarda.

'When a lover comes to her abode, a courtesan should give him a mixture of betel leaves and betel nut, garlands of flowers, and

A public woman, endowed with a good disposition, beauty and who excels in the art of Kamasutra, obtains the title of a Ganika, or courtesan of high quality. She receives a seat of honour in an assemblage of men, respected by the king, and praised by learned men, and she becomes an object of universal regard

By having sex with men courtesan not only gets sexual pleasure but also a maintenance, when she treats the man with love her action is natural; but when the purpose is of milking his wealth, her action is artificial. In the paintings on this page one can see two men showering their affection on the same courtesan while on opposite page two courtesans are taking care of the same client

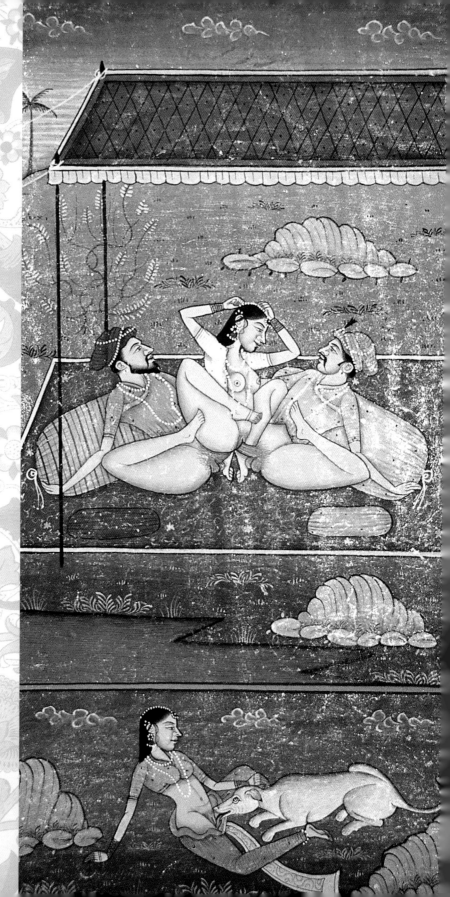

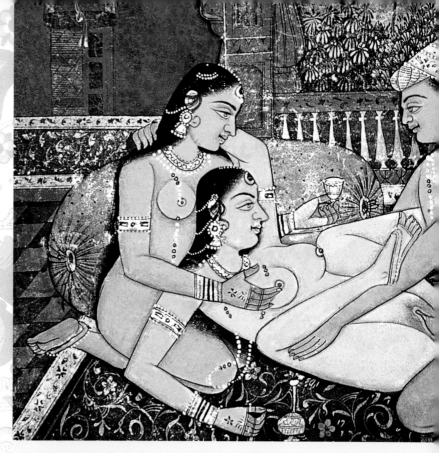

perfumed ointments and showing her skill in arts, should entertain him with a long conversation. She should also give him some loving presents, and make an exchange of her own things with his, and at the same time should show him her skill in sexual enjoyment. When a courtesan is thus united with her lover she should always delight him by affectionate gifts, by conversation, and by the application of tender means of enjoyment.'

LIVING LIKE A WIFE

When a courtesan is living as a wife with her lover, she should behave like a chaste woman, and do everything to his satisfaction. Her duty in this respect, in short is that she should give him pleasure, but should not become attached to him, though behaving as if she were really attached.

She should have a mother dependent on her, one who should be represented as very harsh, and who looked upon money as her chief object in life. In the event of there being no mother, then an old and confidential nurse should play the same role. The mother or nurse,

courtesan

on their part, should appear to be displeased with the lover, and forcibly take her away from him. The woman herself should always show pretended anger, dejection, fear, and shame on this account, but should not disobey the mother or nurse at any time.

She should make out to the mother or nurse that the man is suffering from bad health, and make this a pretext to see him, She is, moreover, to do the following things for the purpose of gaining the man's favour: Sending her female attendant to bring the flowers used by him on the previous day, in order that she may use them herself as a mark of affection, also asking for the mixture of betel nut and leaves that have remained uneaten by him; expressing wonder at his knowledge of sexual intercourse, and the several means of enjoyment used by him; learning from him the sixty-four kinds of pleasure; continually practising the ways of enjoyment as taught by him, and according to his liking; telling him her own desires and secrets; never neglecting him on the bed when he turns his face towards her; touching any parts of his body according to his wish; kissing and embracing him when he is asleep; looking at him with apparent anxiety when he is wrapt in thought; showing neither

When a courtesan is living as a wife with her lover, she should fulfil all his sexual fantasies and do every thing to his satisfaction. Her duty in this respect, in short, is to give him pleasure and invite her friends to realize his fantasies

complete shamelessness, nor excessive bashfulness when he meets her, or sees her standing on the terrace of her house from the public road; expressing a curiosity to see his wives; suspecting even the marks and wounds made by herself with her nails and teeth on his body to have been made by some other woman; keeping her love for him unexpressed by words, but showing it by deeds, and signs, and hints; remaining silent when he is asleep, intoxicated, or sick, placing his hand on her loins, bosom and forehead, and falling asleep after feeling the pleasure of his touch.

When the man sets out on a journey, she should make him swear that he will return quickly, and in his absence should put aside her vows of worshipping the deity, and should wear no ornaments except those that are lucky. If the time fixed for his return has passed, she should endeavour to ascertain the real time of his return from omens, from the reports of the people, and from the positions of the planets, the moon and the stars.

When the man does return home she should worship the god 'Kama', and offer oblations to other deities, and having caused a pot filled with water to be brought by her friends, she should perform the worship in honour of the crow who eats the offerings which we make to the manes of deceased relations. After the first visit is over she should ask her lover also to perform certain rites, and this he will do if he is sufficiently attached to her.

Now a man is said to be sufficiently attached to a woman when his love is disinterested; when he has the same object in view as his beloved one; when he is quite free from any suspicions on her account; and when he is indifferent to money with regard to her.

The extent of the love of women is not known, even to those who are the objects of their affection, on account of its subtlety, and on account of the avarice, and natural intelligence of womankind.

Women are hardly ever known in their true light, though they may love men, or become indifferent towards them, may give them delight, or abandon them, or may extract from them all the wealth that they may possess.

MILKING THE LOVERS' WEALTH

Money is got out of a lover in two ways: by natural or lawful means and by artifices. Old authors are of opinion that when a cour-

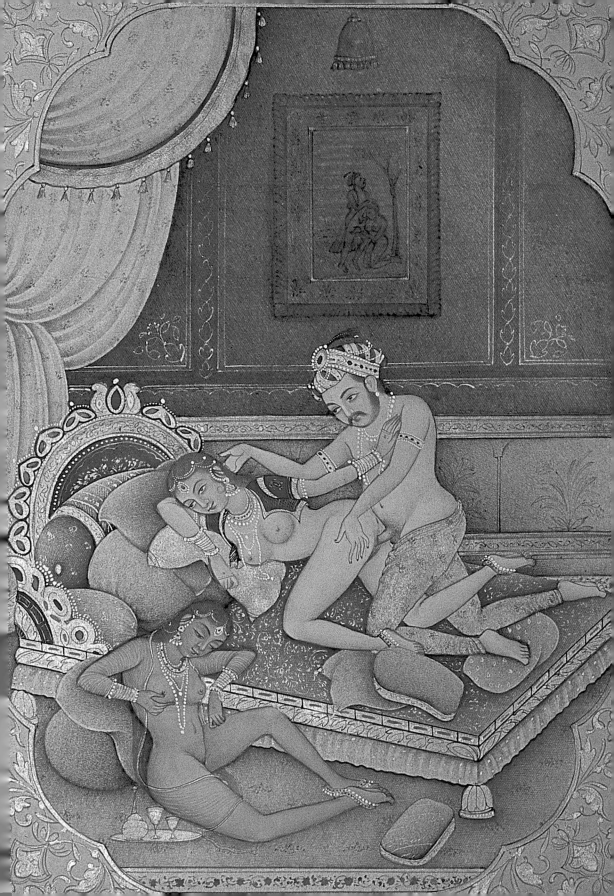

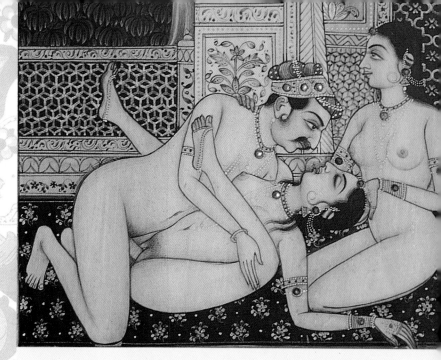

When the daughter of
a courtesan arrives at
the age of puberty,
the mother should get
to gather suitors of
same disposition as
her and tell them that
her daughter will be
deflowered by the
highest bidder

tesan can get as much money as she wants from her lover, she should not make use of artifice. But Vatsyayana lays down that though she may get some money from him by natural means, yet when she makes use of artifice he gives her doubly more, and therefore artifice should be resorted to for the purpose of extorting money from him at all events. There are various ways of doing so.

For instance taking money from him on different occasions, for the purpose of purchasing various articles, such as ornaments, food, drink, flowers, perfumes and clothes, and either not buying them, or getting from him more than their cost; praising his intelligence to his face; pretending to be obliged to make gifts on occasion of festivals connected with vows, trees, gardens, temples, or tanks; pretending that at the time of going to his house, her jewels have been stolen either by the king's guards, or by robbers; alleging that her property has been destroyed by fire, by the falling of her house, or by the carelessness of her servants; pretending to have lost the ornaments of her lover along with her own.

In fact, any excuse is good enough. All a courtesan must remember is that she must sound sincere and honest about her distress at some loss or the other.

A woman should always know the state of the mind, of the feelings, and of the disposition of her lover towards her from the changes of his temper, his manner, and the colour of his face.

Love does not last forever. The behaviour of a waning lover is

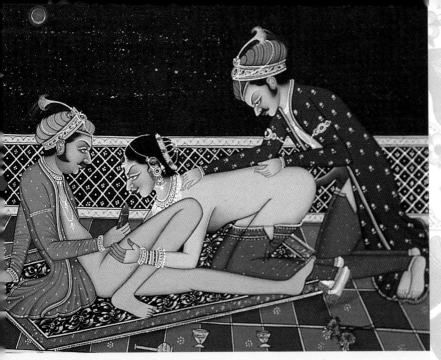

as follows: He gives the woman either less than is wanted, or something else than that which is asked for. He keeps her in hopes in abeyance. He pretends to do one thing and does something else. He does not fulfil her desires. He forgets his promises or does something else than that which he has promised. He speaks with his own servants in a mysterious way. He sleeps in some other house under the pretence of having to do something for a friend. Lastly, he speaks in private with the attendants of a woman with whom he was formerly acquainted.

Now when a courtesan finds that her lover's disposition towards her is changing, she should get possession of all his best things before he becomes aware of her intentions, and allow a supposed creditor to take them away forcibly from her in satisfaction of some pretended debt. After this, if the lover is rich, and has always behaved well towards her, she should ever treat him with respect; but if he is poor and destitute, she should get rid of him as if she had never been acquainted with him in anyway before.

The means of getting rid of a lover are as follows: Describing the habits and vices of the lover as disagreeable and censurable, with the sneer of the lip, and the stamp of the foot. Speaking on a subject with which he is not acquainted; showing no appreciation for his learning, and in fact running him down; seeking the company of men who are superior to him in learning and wisdom; expressing dissatisfaction at the ways and means of enjoyment used by him;

When the daughter of the courtesan is married to the highest bidder, the ties of the marriage are observed only for one year, after that it is the free will of the courtesan to go with whom she likes. If her former lover invites her during this period she should not care about the money of present provider and spend the night with him

not giving him her mouth to kiss; refusing access to her jaghana, i.e. the part of the body between the navel and the thighs; not pressing close up against him at the time when he embraces her; keeping her limbs without movement at the time of congress; desiring him to enjoy her when he is fatigued. In short, leaving him cold and indifferent to his thoughts and feelings

'The duty of a courtesan consists in forming connections with suitable men after due and full consideration, and attaching the person with whom she is united to herself; in obtaining wealth from the person who is attached to her, and then dismissing him after she has taken away all his possessions.'

'A courtesan leading in this manner the life of a wife is not troubled with too many lovers, and yet obtains abundance of wealth.'

REUNION WITH A FORMER LOVER

When a courtesan abandons her lover after all his wealth is exhausted, she may then consider returning to him only if he has acquired fresh wealth, or is still wealthy, and is still attached to her. If this man be living with some other woman then she should think it over.

If the man has been associated with two women and left both women of his own accord, he should not be resorted to, on account of the fickleness of his mind. As regards the man who may have been driven away from both women, if he has been driven away from the last one because the woman could get more money from some other man, then he should be resorted to, for if attached to the first woman he would give her more money, through vanity and emulation to spite the other woman. But if he has been driven away by the woman on account of his poverty, or stinginess, he should be avoided.

In the case of the man who may have left the one woman of his own accord, and been driven away by the other, if he agrees to return to the former and give her plenty of money beforehand, then he should be considered.

In the case of the man who may have left the one woman of his own accord, and be living with another woman, the former (wishing to take up with him again) should first ascertain if he left her in the first instance in the hope of finding some particular quality in the other woman, and that not having found any such quality, he was willing to come back to her, and to give her much money on account of his conduct, and on account of his affection still existing for her.

courtesan

Unlike other temples
of India that are
made out of granite or
sandstone, Hoysala
temples, dating back
to the twelfth century,
are made with softer
dark grey green
chlorite schist, which
is conducive to fine
carving and hardens
with the passage of
time. The details of
the sculptures such as
the one of the lady
holding a parrot are
simply exquisite.
So minute are the
carvings that, the
bracelet of this
heavenly dancer
is free to rotate on
her wrist.

Or, whether having discovered many faults in the other woman, he would now see even more qualities in her than actually exist, and would be prepared to give her much money for these. Or, lastly, to consider whether he was a weak man, or a man fond of enjoying many women, or one who liked a poor woman, or one who never did anything for the woman that he was with. After maturely considering all these things, she should resort to him or not, according to circumstances.

As regards the man who may have been driven away from the one woman, and left the other of his own accord, the former woman (wishing to reunite with him) should first ascertain whether he still has any affection for her, and would consequently spend much money upon her; or whether, being attached to her excellent qualities, he did not take delight in any other woman; or whether, being driven away from her formerly before completely satisfying his sexual desires, he wished to get back to her, so as to be revenged for the injury done to him; or whether he wished to create confidence in her mind, and then take back from her the wealth which she formerly took from him, and finally destroy her; or, lastly, whether he wished first to separate her from her present lover, and then to break away from her himself. If, after considering all these things, she feels that his intentions are really pure and honest, she can reunite herself with him. But if his mind is tainted with evil intentions, he should be avoided.

When a courtesan is resolved to take up again with a former lover, her servants should tell him that his former expulsion from the woman's house was caused by the wickedness of her mother; that the woman loved him just as much as ever at that time, but could not help the occurrence on account of her deference to her mother's will; that she hated the union of her present lover, and disliked him excessively.

When a woman has to choose between two lovers, one of whom was formerly united with her, while the other is a stranger, the Acharyas (sages) are of opinion that the first one is preferable, because his disposition and character being already known by previous careful observation, he can be easily pleased and satisfied; but Vatsyayana thinks that a former lover, having already spent a great deal of his wealth, is not able or willing to give much money again, and is not therefore to be relied upon so much as a stranger.

According to Vatsyayana, a courtesan should be beautiful and amiable, with auspicious body marks. She should have a liking for well-mannered wealthy people. She should take delight in sexual unions with the men of her own status

Particular cases may however arise differing from this general rule on account of the different natures of men.

'Reunion with a former lover may be desirable so as to separate some particular woman from some particular man, or some particular man from some particular woman, or to have a certain effect upon the present lover.'

'When a man is excessively attached to a woman, he is afraid of her coming into contact with other men; he does not then regard or notice her faults and he gives her much wealth through fear of her leaving him.'

'A courtesan should be agreeable to the man who is attached to her, and despise the man who does not care for her. If while she is liv-

A daughter of a courtesan is getting ready for her first night. An enormous amount of money is demanded for such deflowering ritual. In the mirror, she is examining her firm breasts, which are her vital assets

ing with one man, a messenger comes to her from some other man, she may either refuse to listen to any negotiations on his part, or appoint a fixed time for him to visit her, but she should not leave the man who may be living with her and who may be attached to her.'

'A wise woman should only renew her connection with a former lover, if she is satisfied that good fortune, gain, love, and friendship are likely to be the result of such a reunion.'

DIFFERENT KINDS OF GAIN

When a courtesan makes a lot of money everyday, because of many customers, she should not confine herself to a single lover;

A wall painting from South India shows the bull getting excited by the sight of well-endowed rider who is sensually holding on to his horn

under such circumstances, she should fix her rate for one night, after considering the place, the season, and the financial condition of the people, and having regard to her own good qualities and good looks, and after comparing her rates with those of other courtesans. She can inform her lovers, and friends, and acquaintances about these charges. If, however, she can obtain a great gain from a single lover, she may resort to him alone, and live with him like a wife.

Now the sages are of opinion that, when a courtesan has the chance of an equal gain from two lovers at the same time, a preference should be given to the one who would give her the kind of thing which she wants. But Vatsyayana says that the preference should be given to the one who gives her gold, because it cannot be taken back like some other things, it can be easily received, and is also the means of procuring anything that may be wished for. Of such things as gold, silver, copper, bell metal, iron, pots, furniture, beds, upper garments, under vestments, fragrant substances, vessels made of gourds, ghee, oil, corn, cattle, and other things of a like nature, the first - gold - is superior to all the others.

courtesan

This frieze, executed in marble, adorns the entrance of the Jain Temple at Ranakpur. Such erotic carvings were often put to ward off the goddess of lightning who is considered to be a virgin and shies away from the buildings where there is explicit depiction of sex

When the same labour is required to gain any two lovers, or when the same kind of thing is to be got from each of them, the choice should be made by the advice of a friend, or it may be made from their personal qualities, or from the signs of good or bad fortune that may be connected with them.

When there are two lovers, one of whom is attached to the courtesan, and the other is simply very generous, the sages say that the preference should be given to the generous lover, but Vatsyayana is of opinion that the one who is really attached to the courtesan should be preferred, because he can be made to be generous, even as a miser gives money if he becomes fond of a woman, but a man who is simply generous cannot be made to love with real attachment. But among those who are attached to her, if there is one who is poor, and one who is rich, the preference is of course to be given to the latter.

When there are two lovers, one of whom is generous, and the other ready to do any service for the courtesan, some sages say that the one who is ready to do the service should be preferred.

c o u r t e s a n

But Vatsyayana is of opinion that a man who does a service thinks that he has gained his object when he has done something once, but a generous man does not care for what he has given before. Even here the choice should be guided by the likelihood of the future good to be derived from her union with either of them.

When one of the two lovers is grateful, and the other liberal, some sages say that the liberal one should be preferred, but Vatsyayana is of opinion that the former should be chosen, because liberal men are generally haughty, out spoken and have little consideration for others. Even though these liberal men have been on friendly terms for a long time, yet if they see any fault in the courtesan or are told lies about her by some other woman, they do not care for past services, and leave abruptly. On the other hand the grateful man does not at once break off from her, on account of a regard for the pains she may have taken to please him. In this case also the choice is to be guided with respect to what may happen in future.

c o u r t e s a n

When an occasion for complying with the request of a friend and a chance of getting money come together, the sages say that the chance of getting money should be preferred. Vatsyayana thinks that the money can be obtained tomorrow as well as today, but in making the final choice, due consideration should be given to money.

When the chance of getting money and the chance of avoiding some disaster come at the same time, the sages are of opinion that the chance of getting money should be preferred. But Vatsyayana says that money has only a limited importance, while a disaster that is once averted may never occur again. Here, however, the choice should be guided by the greatness or small-ness of the disaster.

The gains of the wealthiest and best kind of courtesans are to be spent as follows: building temples, tanks, and gardens; giving a thousand cows to different Brahmins; carrying on the worship of the Gods, and celebrating festivals in their honour; and lastly, performing such vows as may be within their means.

Having a white dress to wear every day; getting sufficient food and drink to satisfy hunger and thirst; eating daily a perfumed tambula, i.e. a mixture of betel nut and betel leaves; and wearing ornaments gilt with gold. The sages say that these represent the gains of all the middle and lower classes of courtesans, but Vatsyayana is of opinion that their gains cannot be calculated, or fixed in any way, as these depend on the influence of the place, the customs of the people, their own appearance, and many other things.

When a courtesan wants to keep some particular man from some other woman; or wishes to get him away from some woman to whom he may be attached or to deprive some woman of the gains realized by her from him; for any of the above reasons, she should agree to take from him only a small sum of money in a friendly way.

When a courtesan intends to abandon a particular lover, and take up with another one; or that having squandered all his money, and become penniless, his father would come and take him away; or that her lover is about to lose his position or, she should, under any of these circumstances, endeavour to get as much money as she can from him as soon as possible.

(Following pages)
In Gramaneri many young men enjoy a woman that may be married to one of them, either one after the other or all at the same time. The same thing can be done when many men sitting with a courtesan start to enjoy her. Women can also do the same to a man who they accidentally get hold of in the harem

'In considering her present gains, and her future welfare,
a courtesan should avoid such persons as have gained their means of subsistence
with very great difficulty, as also those who have become selfish
and hard-hearted by becoming the favourites of kings.'
'She should make every endeavour to unite herself with prosperous and well-to-do
people, and with those whom it is dangerous to avoid,
or to slight in any way.
Even at some cost to herself she should become acquainted with
energetic and liberal-minded men,
who when pleased would give her a large sum of money,
even for very little service, or for some small thing.'

love potion

THE MEANS OF INCREASING THE LOVELINESS OF A PERSON IN THE EYES OF OTHERS.

When a person fails to obtain the object of his desires by the ways mentioned previously, then he should use other means. Good looks, good qualities, youth, and liberality are the most natural means of making a person attractive in the eyes of others. But in the absence of these a man or a woman must have resort to artificial means, or to art, and the following are some recipes that may be found useful.

An ointment made of the tabernamontana coronaria, the costus speciosus or arabicus, and the flacourtia cataphracta, can be used as an ointment of adornment.

If a fine powder is made of the above plants, and applied to the wick of a lamp, which is made to burn with the oil of blue vitrol, the black pigment or lamp black produced there when applied to the eyelashes, has the effect of making a person look lovely.

The oil of the hogweed, the echites putescens, the sarina plant, the yellow amaranth, and the leaf of the nymphae, if applied to the body, has the same effect.

By eating the powder of the nelumbrium speciosum, the blue lotus, and the mesna roxburghii, with ghee (clarified butter) and honey, a man becomes lovely in the eyes of others.

If the bone of a peacock or of a hyena be covered with gold, and tied on the right hand, it makes a man lovely in the eyes of other people.

In the same way, if a bead, made of the seed of the jujube, or of the conch shell, be enchanted by the incantations mentioned in the Atharvana Veda, or by the incantations of those well skilled in the science of magic, and tied on the hand, it produces the same result as described above.

When a female attendant arrives at the age of puberty, her master should keep her secluded, and when men ardently desire her on account of her seclusion, and on account of the difficulty of approaching her, he should then bestow her hand on such a person as may endow her with wealth and happiness.

The followers of some Tantaric cult collected the love juices when the yogis meditated in the positions of Kamasutra. These drops were considered sacred by the followers of the cult

love potion

When the daughter of a courtesan arrives at the age of puberty, the mother should get together a lot of young men of the same age, disposition, and knowledge as her daughter, and tell them that she would give her in marriage to the person who would give her expensive presents.

After this the daughter should be kept in seclusion as far as possible, and the mother should give her in marriage to the man who may be ready to give her the presents as demanded. If the mother is unable to get so much out of the man, she should show some of her own things as having been given to the daughter by the bridegroom.

The daughter, too, should make herself attractive to the sons of wealthy men, unknown to her mother, and make them attracted to her. She should meet them at the time of learning to sing, in places where music is played and at

love potion

If a man, after
anointing his lingam
with a mixture of the
powders of the white
thorn apple, the long
pepper, black pepper
and honey, engages in
sexual union with a
woman, he makes her
slave of his will

the houses of other people. Later, she should ask her mother,
to be allowed to unite with the man who is most agreeable
to her.

When the daughter of a courtesan is thus given to a man, the
ties of marriage should be observed for one year, and after that
she may do what she likes. Even after the end of the year, when
otherwise engaged, if she is invited by her first husband to come
and see him, she should put aside her present lover, and go to
him for the night.

These are some examples of temporary marriage among
courtesans, and of increasing their loveliness, and their value in
the eyes of others. What has been said about them also
applies to the daughters of dancing women, whose mothers
should give them only to such persons as are likely to become
useful to them in various ways.

love potion

THE WAYS OF SUBJUGATING OTHERS
TO ONE'S OWN WILL

If a man, after anointing his lingam with a mixture of the powders of the white thorn apple, the long pepper and, the black pepper, and honey, engages in sexual union with a woman, he makes her subject to his will.

The application of a mixture of the leaf of the plant vatodbhranta, of the flowers thrown on a human corpse when carried out to be burnt, and the powder of the bones of the peacock, and of the jiwanjiva bird produces the same effect. The remains of a kite who has died a natural death, ground into powder, and mixed with cowach and honey, has also the same effect. Anointing oneself with an ointment made of the plant emblica myrabolans has the power of subjecting women to one's will.

If a man cuts into small pieces the sprouts of the vajnasunhi plant, and dips them into a mixture of red arsenic and sulphur, and then dries them seven times, and applies this powder mixed with honey to his lingam, he can subjugate a woman to his will directly that he has had sexual union with her, or if, by burning these very sprouts at night and looking at the smoke, he sees a golden moon behind, he will then be successful with any woman; or if he throws some of the powder of these same sprouts mixed with the excrement of a monkey upon a maiden, she will not be given in marriage to anybody else.

If pieces of the arris root are dressed with the oil of the mango, and placed for six months in a hole made in the trunk of the sisu tree, and are then taken out and made up into an ointment, and applied to the lingam, this is said to serve as the means of subjugating women.

If the bone of a camel is dipped into the juice of the plant eclipta prostata, and then burnt, and the black pigment produced from its ashes is placed in a box also made of the bone of a camel, and applied to the eye lashes with a pencil also made of the bone of a camel, then that pigment serves as a means of subjugating others to the person who uses it. The same effect can be produced by black pigment made of the bones of hawks, vultures, and peacocks.

love potion

As the age increases man's virility declines. Here one can see an old barber, who shaving a concubine, is not aroused by the nature of his work. Drinking milk mixed with sugar, and having testicle of a ram or goat boiled in it helps increase the vigour of the man

THE MEANS OF INCREASING SEXUAL VIGOUR

A man obtains sexual vigour by drinking milk mixed with sugar, the root of the uchchata plant, the piper chaba, and liquorice.

Drinking milk, mixed with sugar, and having the testicle of a ram or a goat boiled in it, is also productive of vigour.

The drinking of the juice of the hedysarum gangeticum, the kuili, and the kshirika plant mixed with milk, produces the same effect.

love potion

If a man notices that his lover is not satisfied, that she keeps throwing her head around and begs him to continue, in such cases man should use his fingers and tongue on her yoni to satisfy her

In the opinion of Guru Babhravya, the Apadravyas (things that are put on around the lingam to supplement its length or thickness, so as to fit the yoni) should be made out of gold, ivory or from different kinds of wood. These should be soft, cool and provocative of sexual vigour and well fitted to serve the intended purpose

According to ancient authors, if a man pounds the seeds or roots of the trapa bispinosa, the kasurika, the tuscan jasmine, and liquorice, together with the kshirakapoli (a kind of onion), and puts the powder into milk mixed with sugar and ghee, and having boiled the whole mixture on a moderate fire, drinks the paste so formed, he will be able to enjoy innumerable women.

In the same way, if a man mixes rice with the eggs of the sparrow, and having boiled this in milk, adds to it ghee and honey, and drinks as much of it as necessary, this will increase sexual power and potency.

If a man takes the outer covering of sesamum seeds, and soaks them with the eggs of sparrows, and then, having boiled them in milk, mixed with sugar and ghee, along with the fruits

love potion

of the trapa bispinosa and the kasurika plant, and adding to it the flour of wheat and beans, and then drinks this composition, he is said to be able to enjoy many women.

If ghee, honey, sugar and liquorice in equal quantities, the juice of the fennel plant, and milk are mixed together, this nectar-like composition is said to be holy, and provocative of sexual vigour, a preservative of life, and sweet to the taste.

Drinking boiled ghee, or clarified butter, in the morning during the spring season, is said to be beneficial to health and strength and agreeable to the taste.

'The mean of producing love and sexual vigour should be learnt from the science of medicine, from the Vedas, from those who are learned in the arts of magic, and from confidential relatives. No means should be tried which are doubtful in their effects, which are likely to cause injury to the body, which involve the death of animals, and which bring us in contact with impure things. Such means should only be used as are holy, acknowledged to be good, and approved of by Brahmins and friends.'

love potion

Dance was an important part of the life of pleasure seeking citizen. Here one can see a guru imparting dance lessons in a tenth century sculpture on the lower walls of Laxmana Temple in Khajuraho

APADRAVYAS (SEX ORNAMENTS)

If a man is unable to satisfy a Hastini, or Elephant woman, he should have recourse to various means to excite her passion. At the beginning he should rub her yoni with his hand or fingers, and not begin to have intercourse with her until she becomes excited, or experiences pleasure.

Or, he may make use of certain Apadravyas, or things which are put on or around the lingam to supplement its length or its thickness, so as to fit it to the yoni. In the opinion of Babhravya, these Apadravyas should be made of gold, silver, copper, iron, ivory, buffalo's horn, various kinds of wood, and should be soft, cool, provocative of sexual vigour, and well fitted to serve the intended purpose.

THE FOLLOWING ARE THE DIFFERENT KINDS OF APADRAVYAS (SEX ORNAMENTS)

The Armlet (Valaya) should be of the same size as the lingam,

love potion

and should have its outer surface made rough with globules. The Bracelet (Chudaka) is made by joining three or more armlets, until they come up to the required length of the lingam. The single bracelet is formed by wrapping a single wire around the lingam, according to its dimensions.

The Kantuka or Jalaka is a tube open at both ends, with a hole through it, outwardly rough and studded with soft globules, and made to fit the side of the yoni, and tied to the waist. When such a tube is not available, then a tube made of the wood apple, or tubular stalk of the bottle gourd, or a reed made soft with oil and extracts of plants, and tied to the waist with strings, should be made use of. These can also be used in place of the lingam.

The people of the southern countries think that true sexual pleasure cannot be obtained without perforating the lingam, and they therefore cause it to be pierced like the lobes of the ears of an infant pierced for earrings.

A young man should perforate his lingam with the help of a sharp instrument, and then stand in water so long as the blood continues to flow. At night, he should engage in sexual intercourse, even with vigour, so as to clean the hole. After this he should continue to wash the hole with decoctions, and increase the size by putting into it small pieces of cane or fruit stalks of the simapatra plant, and thus gradually enlarge the orifice. It may also be washed with liquorice mixed with honey and the hole should also be anointed with a small quantity of oil.

In the hole made in the lingam a man may put Apadravyas of various forms, such as the 'round', the 'round on one side', the 'wooden mortar', the 'flower', the 'armlet', the 'bone of the heron', the 'goad of the elephant', the 'collection of eight balls', the 'lock of hair', the 'place where four roads meet', and other things named according to their forms and means of using them. All these Apadravyas should be rough on the outside according to their requirements.

When a man wishes to enlarge his lingam, he should rub it with the bristles of certain insects that live in trees, and then, after rubbing it for ten nights with oils. By continuing to do this a swelling will be gradually produced in the lingam, and he

To increase the vigour
during the sexual
intercourse
Kamasutra advises
to take various
aphrodisiacs so that
the duration
of enjoyment can be
prolonged to satisfy
both partners

213

should then lie face down on a cot, and hang down his lingam through a hole in the cot. After this he should take away all the pain from the swelling by using cool concoctions. The swelling, which is called 'Suka', lasts for life.

The enlargement of the lingam is also effected by rubbing it or moistening it with oil boiled on a moderate fire along with the seeds of the pomegranate, and the cucumber, the juices of the valuka plant, the hastri-charma plant and the eggplant.

LOVE SPELLS

If a man mixes the powder of the milk hedge plant, and the kantaka plant with the excrement of a monkey and the powdered root of the lanjalika plant, and throws this mixture on a woman, she will not love anybody else afterwards.

If a man thickens the juice of the fruits of the cassia fistula, and the eugenia jambolana by mixing them with the powder of the soma plant, the vernonia anthelmintica, the eclipta prostata, and the lohopa-jihirka, and applies this composition to the yoni of a woman, and then has sexual intercourse with her, his love for her will be destroyed.

The same effect is produced if a man has connection with a woman who has bathed in the buttermilk of a she-buffalo mixed with the powders of the gopalika plant, the banu-padika plant and the yellow amaranth.

An ointment made of the flowers of the nauclea cadamba, the hog plum, and the eugenia jambolana, and used by a woman, causes her to be disliked by her husband. Garlands made of these flowers, when worn by the woman, produce the same effect.

An ointment made of the fruit of the asteracantha longifolia will contract the yoni of a Hastini or Elephant woman, and this contraction lasts for one night.

An ointment made by pounding the roots of the nelumbrium speciosum, and of the blue lotus, and the powder of the plant physalis flexuosa mixed with ghee and honey, will enlarge the yoni of the Mrigi or Deer woman.

A woman who hears a man playing on a reed pipe which has been dressed with the juices of the bahupadika plant, becomes his slave.

If a man is unable to satisfy a Hastini, or Elephant woman, he should have recourse to various means to excite her passion. At the beginning he should rub her yoni with his hand or fingers, and not begin to have intercourse with her until she becomes excited

Vatsyayana's Conclusion

'Thus have I written in a few words the "Science of love", after reading the texts of ancient authors, and following the ways of enjoyment mentioned in them.'

'He who is acquainted with the true principles of this science pays regard to Dharma, Artha, Kama, and to his own experiences, as well as to the teachings of others, and does not act simply on the dictates of his own desire.

As for the errors in the science of love which I have mentioned in this work, on my own authority as an author, I have, immediately after mentioning them, carefully censured and prohibited them.'

An act is never looked upon with indulgence for the simple reason that it is authorised by the science, because it ought to be remembered that it is the intention of the science, that the rules which it contains should only be acted upon in particular cases. After reading and considering the works of Babhravya and other ancient authors, and thinking over the meaning of the rules given by them, the Kamasutra was composed, according to the precepts of Holy Writ, for the benefit of the world, by Vatsyayana, while leading the life of a religious student, and wholly engaged in the contemplation of the Deity.'

'This work is not intended to be used merely as an instrument for satisfying our desires. A person, acquainted with the true principles of this science, and who preserves his Dharma, Artha, and Kama, and has regard for the practices of the people, is sure to obtain the mastery over his senses.'

'In short, an intelligent and prudent person, attending to Dharma and Artha, and attending to Kama also, without becoming the slave of his passions, obtains success in everything that he may undertake.'